Never Retreat
(Mai Daur)

Antonio Ferrante di Ruffano

Translated by Chris Ferrante di Ruffano

The Private Library
London

Published in October 2010 by: The Private Library, 15 Pendrell House, New Compton Street, London WC2H 8DF.

Printed by Lulu.com.

Vita Vissuta, on which *Never Retreat* is based, was published in Italian by Editions Clepsydre, 1117 Alsembergsteenweg, 1650 Beersel, Belgium, in 2004.

ISBN: 978-0-9566775-0-1

FOREWORD

I WAS ALREADY acquainted with some chapters in the battles fought by Lieutenant of the Alpini Marchese Antonio Ferrante di Ruffano, president of the Retired Italian Officers in Belgium, when I had the opportunity to meet him in Brussels where I had been posted as Italian representative to NATO. This offered me the chance to get to know him and to appreciate both his heroic past as a Second World War combatant and his dedication as a civil servant in the capital of the European Union. I became his confidant and friend.

It is therefore with pleasure that I have learned he has completed this account of his adventurous life to leave a documented record not only to his family and descendants, but to his friends, to historians and to those exploring real-life stories lived on the ground among our soldiers rather than in the more rarefied atmosphere of high command. His record is also left to the Julia Brigade, successor to the heroic division of the same name that repeatedly sacrificed itself for king and country. However, this book is dedicated above all to Lieut Ferrante's Alpini, to those few veterans still alive and to the families of those who have preceded him to heaven.

In the immediate aftermath of the war I chose as my career that of officer in the Italian army. This choice was motivated by passion, by the love for my country that I had felt since childhood, and also by wanting to redeem the honour of the Italian army after the events of September 1943. My job is the only in human endeavour in which we prepare for a lifetime of going to war but with the ultimate goal of trying to prevent it. During my career I have at times asked myself if, when tested in combat, I would have kept the calmness and self-control necessary to reach the best decisions in pursuit of an objective while trying to reduce the risk to my men, especially if I had been wounded. I was a child during the war and so not old enough for active combat, as had several friends and relatives on fronts both on land and sea. But my long career in the forces has enabled me to derive a positive answer to my question and also to realise that Antonio Ferrante di Ruffano was a "great commander". He was a charismatic leader while also being effective tactically and operationally.

Heroism, however, is something different. Heroism consists of taking up a challenge, conscious or not, for reasons of duty, of dignity, of truth to values, of love, or of measuring up to others in fighting against difficulties, adversities and the enemy, even all three. Heroism occurs in the pursuit of achieving something intrinsically good. It is a value considered supreme, but which can also require the ultimate sacrifice. In this light, the long life of Marchese Ferrante di Ruffano has been, in my opinion, a conscious, continuous and heroic challenge against death.

This was evident in everything from when he started wearing the Italian colours at the Olympic Games and when he tore the flag from the tower of a French fort after a perilous climb (a feat that matched the most daring actions carried out in the conquering of Monte Nero during the First World War). The same can be said of the desperate days when he contributed towards pushing back the many assaults of the Greek army in the high mountains of Albania, of the stormy night when he saved himself and other Alpini from the sinking *Galilea,* and of the battles on the Don in Russia, at Christmas time in 1942. During the latter, after fighting Soviet tanks in freezing conditions with only light weapons, he was severely wounded in the head, pronounced dead and placed among a stack of corpses in front of the field hospital. Last but not least, his challenge to death is evident in his dramatic transfer to Soviet concentration camps and his long stays there as a POW. He struggled to survive hunger, cruelty and the psychological and political intimidation of the Soviet camp guards.

When he returned home, Lieut Ferrante found himself facing yet another moral challenge: whether to remain loyal to the oath that, as an officer, he had made to his king, or to continue his military career under the Italian republic. Once again, he made the more uncomfortable choice, remaining true to his values and giving up his military career. Nevertheless, as a civil servant he has continued to support and defend the ideal of his fatherland and its honour in foreign lands, even when the weight of defeat still rested heavily on the shoulders of the Italian people and especially of those combatants who chose to remain faithful to their sovereign.

And he still rises to the challenge of addressing the omissions of history. On 4th November every year, a day celebrating victory and the armed forces, he goes to the graves of our First World War soldiers buried in Belgium and, removing the little modern Italian flags, replaces them with little royalist ones. It was for that flag that they fought and sacrificed their lives.

I welcome therefore, among the recollections of a tormented and courageous past, the memories of Lieutenant of the Alpini Marchese Antonio Ferrante di Ruffano. In peace, as in war, he has honoured Italy, the army and the Alpini in particular. He has also honoured his family name and above all *truth*. He will remain an example to present and future generations.

He would have deserved the highest military award, but fate has chosen to reward him instead with good health, enabling him to continue his long, adventurous and courageous life.

My heartfelt compliments, my dear Ferrante, and best wishes for further victorious challenges.

Rome, 18th June 2004
Generale Corpo d'Armata (Lieut. Gen)
Ing. Vittorio Bernard
Head of the Italian Military Delegation to NATO
President Nat. Assoc. Sappers of Italy

TRANSLATOR'S NOTE

I FIRST REMEMBER hearing of the people and events described in *Never Retreat* as a boy of four or five, asking my father about the war and how he acquired the scars on the left side of his face. I listened with a sense of wonder and of pride, pressing him for facts but careful not to irritate him. The more I heard, the more I wanted to know.

This story has remained with me and the interest has, if anything, increased. I still remember my father taking me to reunions of his Alpini veterans, carrying me on his shoulders. In time, I got to meet some of the men who feature in *Never Retreat*, such as Padre Don Brevi who, during a Russian offensive and with his position about to be overwhelmed, decided that the life of his men came before his religious beliefs. Manning a heavy machine-gun, he kept the enemy in check until reinforcements arrived, inflicting severe losses. Or Alpino Viezzi, who after single-handedly destroying a Russian T34 tank marched for two days with his eyeball hanging from the optical nerve on his cheek until he reached safety.

Nearly all these men are now dead. My father always said that the outside world could never comprehend what the combatants experienced during that war and even more during their captivity in Soviet concentration camps. However, in 2004 at the age of 89 he had a change of heart and wrote this book in Italian. I asked him for his permission to translate it into English, to reach a wider audience, and after some thought he agreed.

In the two years that this translation has taken, my main concern has been to remain faithful to the narrative and to the spirit in which this story is told. History has more than one facet and the more we enquire about how different people experienced events, the more objective we become and less likely to repeat the errors of the past. This book confirms that honour and courage are not the exclusive features of groups or nations, but exist within some human beings and are enhanced by the difficulties thrown across their paths.

It is for these men of courage and honour that I completed this translation. The more I progressed, the more I felt that it is a privilege to be involved in handing these events down to posterity.

There are certain people that I would like to especially thank for their kind assistance. One is Gen Vittorio Bernard, for convincing my father that his story could not be allowed to die with him and for the warm support and encouragement given. Another friend who has also helped with patience and precision in remembering events is Luciano Papinutto, whom my father always calls Papinutti, his old sergeant and friend for almost 70 years who always welcomes us during the last weekend in March, when the commemoration for the sinking of the *Galilea* takes place.

My thanks also go to Alex Martin, who helped me get started in this endeavour in the UK and to a number of friends whom I have utilised to proof-read parts of my text. Lastly, I would especially like to thank Rory O'Callaghan, who has been of enormous assistance in advising the total beginner that I am, editing and reviewing the text and enabling my father and me to have this book printed.

Chris Ferrante di Ruffano

2nd June 2010

A note on the photographs. These were all taken by the author, except that of Figure 9 (the summit of Mount Golico, page 53), using his Leica camera. Although lost now, he recalls that the immensely robust camera was probably a III Series model, with a Summar 50mm 1:2 lens, one of the best cameras available at the time and manufactured from 1937 until the 1950s. He found the Mount Golico picture abandoned, along with many others, in the offices of the Associazione Nazionale Alpini, Milan, many years after the war. It had no name on the print.

The crest on the title page bearing the motto "Mai Daur" is that of the Gemona battalion, with which the author served. "Mai Daur" means "never retreat" in the Friulano dialect of Italian. To quote a phrase of the author, it was a motto "written in blood".

To my old flag

To crushed Italy that will one day resurrect itself

*To all my Alpini who defended her with their honour
and blood*

And, especially, to those remembered in this book

TABLE OF CONTENTS

1: EARLY DAYS

AN ITALIAN ABROAD

I WAS ALMOST born a Turk. I was conceived in Adalia – now Antalya – a large Turkish town on the Mediterranean, where my father had been posted at the start of his career in the Italian diplomatic service. Agostino Ferrante di Ruffano, my father, was of old Neapolitan stock, from a family close to the former King of Naples, while my mother's family – the MacVeagh's – originated in Illinois. They were prominent in the US State Department, with two of her uncles having been the first US ambassadors to China and to Rome.

First, I would like to briefly mention Grandma, Mary Hammond, my mother's mother. She was quite beautiful, but forceful too. She refused to wear glasses, preferring instead to hold a *lorgnette* to her eyes. She had always maintained that her first husband, Lincoln MacVeagh, known to us as Nanuk, had died. However, many years later he reappeared, much to everybody's shock. It emerged that Grandma had not been widowed at all, but had in fact divorced Nanuk after he developed a drinking problem to cope with her demanding personality. Nanuk lost his job and left home, heartbroken, disappearing for many years. He eventually ended up living with a barmaid. Down on his luck and ill, he was finally tracked down by his younger brother Charlie who returned him to the family. Nanuk gave up the drink when he married again, this time to Elisabeth McKeen, whom we came to know as Cousin Bess. They went to live on Jewells Island, off the coast of Maine, where I used to visit them as a child. Nanuk lived out his last years there, quite content at last.

To return to my story, after divorcing Nanuk, Grandma had married the senior American diplomat in Athens. There she was joined by her daughter Virginia, my mother, back from school in Switzerland. Her arrival coincided with a brief visit by my father to Athens, where they met. As my mother spoke no Italian and my father no English, they communicated in French. They continued to do so for the rest of their lives. It was Grandma to whom my father went to ask for her daughter's hand in marriage. After scrutinising him through her *lorgnette*, she pronounced that he should prove acceptable as a husband, because "he was a marquis and had good teeth". She demanded, however, that their first son be named after her pet poodle Tony, whom she adored. Recovering quickly from his surprise, my father agreed. I was the first born and my father, true to his word, named me Antonio, shortened to Tony. I owe my name to a dog.

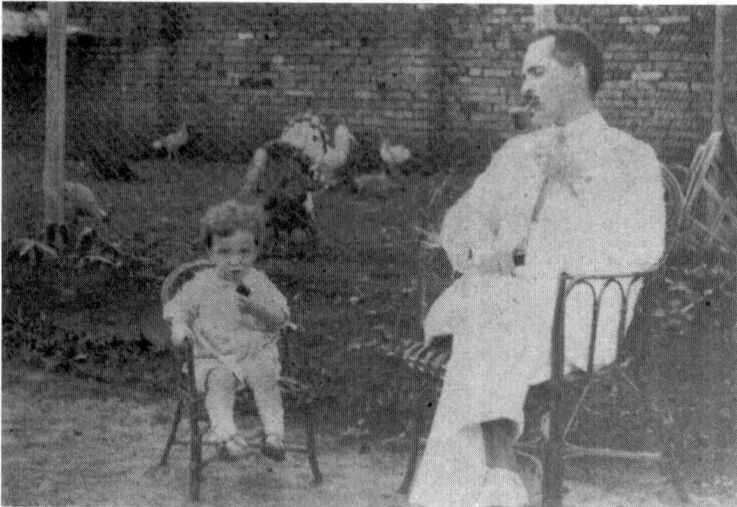

Figure 1: Aged 2, trying to smoke a pipe with my diplomat father in Adalia, Turkey, in 1916

Having been posted to Turkey, my parents had to leave shortly before the start of the First World War and I was born in Florence, in July 1914. We returned to Adalia that September for a time, then again after the end of the war in 1919. By then the Ottoman Empire had ceased to exist and had been replaced in the region by modern Turkey. My father's main instructions, as vice-consul, were to gain the confidence of the Turkish authorities and to promote Italian interests in the area, countering the influence of the French and the British.

I remember our large house, with rose bushes at the front and a yard with some domestic animals at the back. It also had a garden with banana and apricot trees. I never tasted better apricots. Once, when expecting a guest for dinner, my father caught a chicken and poured a spoonful of brandy down its gullet. The animal started to wobble. "See? He's drunk, he won't feel a thing," my father said. Then he wrung the chicken's neck.

I recall my parents exploring Greek and Roman ruins, to the surprise of the locals who couldn't understand this obscure interest in old stones. They found several artifacts, such as a small but heavy Roman sarcophagus, and a Greek statue in alabaster, 30cm tall. It was probably of Aphrodite but it had no arms. We named her Lucy and gave her a place of honour in our living room, where she remained for many years.

We also had a pet armadillo called Tatu who died but, curiously, remained with us anyway. My parents had him stuffed and he went to join Lucy in the living room.

In Adalia, when I was about four, I decided to run away from home. I packed a small bag and walked into town. After anxious searching, my parents found me sitting on the pavement in front of a sweet stall. I was happily munching on candy sticks.

A couple of years later we moved to Brazil. One day, a pig found its way into our garden and onto our veranda, having somehow gotten hold of our pet canary and eaten it. My father, furious, pulled out his sword, handed me the scabbard, and ordered: "You go there to the left, I'll go to the right! If you see the pig, kill it!" The pig seemed very large to me however, so whenever it ran past I stepped to the side, prudently. Now and then my father appeared, asking: "Well, have you seen it?" "Noooo…" I would reply. "No at all."

Our family increased and I was followed by two sisters and two brothers, born respectively in Brazil, the USA, Canada and Australia, countries where my father was posted during his career.

In 1920 we moved to Boston. I joined the cub scouts and went to Pocasset camp. There we did a lot of hiking, climbing Mount Washington and Rattlesnake Hill. We were also taken to the forest at night and, although initially afraid, my fear receded in the knowledge that I was always close to others. I also passed my swimming test by paddling into the middle of the lake fully clothed in our canoe, tipping it over, getting undressed in the water, emptying the canoe and paddling it back to shore. We were also taught to shoot. At the age of seven I, somewhat inexplicably, received a medal as a marksman from the Winchester gun company. Boxing posed more of a problem because I was still too small and too thin. I often had to step aside in tears.

Throughout those years, I remember my father repeating to me: "You are Italian and you must rise above everyone; you must always strive to be the first, in your studies as in sport. You must never give up". Gradually, this message got through; I acquired confidence, got better and started winning some competitions.

Figure 2: Aged 4, in Malaga, Spain

I was given an allowance of 5 cents a week with which I bought chewing gum or Pepsi-Cola. One time we went to see a movie, the first I saw. It was a silent film featuring Harold Lloyd.

We sometimes spent the months of July and August in Dublin, New Hampshire, the residence of my mother's old uncle Franklin MacVeagh, who invited us. Previously Secretary to the US Treasury under President Taft then a senator, he had settled down with his cows and his stables of ponies on his estate overlooking Dublin Lake. We rented a small house nearby and I remember going to play with my sister and other friends in the ice-house. It was a small construction filled with sawdust, where large blocks of ice cut from the lake in winter were stored ready for use in the houses nearby. Youngsters used to gather on the banks of the lake, entertained occasionally by a Mr Smith. He would float along on a raft, disguised as a large toad.

Our final years in Boston were marked by Prohibition, which affected all Americans. Being a foreign diplomat, my father was exempted and he continued to receive gin and whisky from our embassy in Washington. Without anyone knowing, my father started to produce his own "bathtub gin" – revealing to me the recipe and process – which he then poured into Gordon's gin bottles. Understandably, the Prohibition period was one of great popularity for our house. Visits soared and family friends multiplied, with my parents giving bridge and cocktail parties. As they ended my sister and I used to drink the remaining cocktails and finish the food. And nobody ever found out.

During my time in Boston I observed many indications of broader developments that were modifying American life. New products appeared. In 1921, for example, many cars did not yet have steering wheels, but a longitudinal bar in front of the driver – and a rubber pump horn on the outside. To turn you had to manoeuvre your hand and perform the appropriate gesture. There were no traffic lights on the streets. Tyres were simple and fragile. I can remember my father, more than once, fixing a flat tyre by gluing a piece of rubber on the hole. I also noticed neon lights announcing themselves with garish colours across town, while cellophane and plastic made their quieter arrival before becoming almost indispensable. Many of these things were still unknown in Europe.

Shortly before leaving Boston the financial crash occurred, followed by the Depression. Fortunately, we remained untouched and our house retained that air of prosperity which so many of those around us had suddenly lost. It was a terrible period, with many losing everything and some taking their lives. As a consequence, the number of friends and visitors increased even more.

A LONELY SCHOOLING

AT THE AGE OF 10, my parents decided I had to continue my education in Italy. I travelled from Boston, via Naples, to Rome with my mother and she left me there – we were both in tears – at a religious boarding school. Alone, wrenched from my family at a tender age, in a world unknown to me, this abandoning caused a severe psychological reaction that weighed negatively on me for the rest of my life.

I wore the black uniform of the school and slept in a dormitory with many other pupils. To go to the toilet, we had to go downstairs and cross an open courtyard where, under a lean-to with no walls, the 45 latrines had no seats. Obligatory silence ruled for most of the day. In the basement were six bath-tubs set in concrete. I tried to avoid them as much as I could. They looked like coffins.

The kitchen was disgusting: the fried potatoes came with the odd fried cockroach, the cherries had worms and the small pieces of chocolate given to us around four in the afternoon were a strange colour and tasted like the ivory soap I used to wash myself with in Boston. I often found refuge in the chapel, where a statue of the Virgin gave me comfort.

Given the loss of my parents and friends, it was a lonely four years, leaving me with a great sense of solitude. After that, even though my family always welcomed me with affection on my visits to the US, I felt I never regained the warmth and affection that all of us so badly need during childhood. I realise though that they thought they were acting in my best interests. In those days it was unacceptable that the sons of diplomats were not educated in their country of origin. Today on the other hand, Italian diplomats couldn't care less and often prefer to enroll their children in French or English schools.

During the summer holidays, I used to join my family in Boston. My father wanted me to learn about his duties so, when I was 13, he took me to visit Nicola Sacco and Bartolomeo Vanzetti in prison. The trial and execution of these two alleged Italian anarchists became a *cause célèbre*. They were arrested in 1920 for homicide and executed in 1927, even though the court never managed conclusively to prove their guilt. As the Italian consul in Boston, my father was in contact with both of the accused and became involved in the case, which became a famous miscarriage of justice that reflected badly on the United States. One day, my father took me to their cell and said: "Look at them. These poor people may be immigrants like Al Capone and Lucky Luciano and I would not choose them as friends, but they are Italians. They don't know anything of politics."

When I was 16, my parents moved to Ottawa, in Canada, and then back to Philadelphia. During the summer, with my friend Henry Kurz, I bought an old car. It was red and yellow with a Moon engine but had parts from various other marques. At that age I could legally drive and we hatched a plan to travel to Ottawa and back. "In this heap?" my father asked sarcastically. "It won't travel more than 50 miles." He was so certain that he bet 50 dollars on our anticipated misfortune.

We named the car Bea, after Bea Churchman, a likeable but loud girl in our group, loaded it with camping equipment and food, and set off. Our first stop was at Uncle Hammond and Aunt Emily's house. Astounded by our plan, they donated 50 dollars towards our venture. In the forests of Quebec two of our tyres burst but, despite this and a few other minor problems, we made it to Ottawa. And all the way back. The morning after we got back, all four of Bea's tyres had gone flat. We repaired them and the car and sold it to our girlfriends for 10 dollars, but only on condition that Bea's name would remain unchanged.

In 1932 my father was posted to Sydney, Australia, as consul general for Australasia. We rented a villa owned by an eccentric Englishman in the district of Woolloomooloo (yes, it has eight o's). The villa's most interesting feature was the bathroom. The shower shot water from the top and the sides, and the lighting could be changed from white to red or blue. The tub was encased in the floor and its sides formed the sides of tropical fish tanks, whose denizens gazed curiously as we humans soaked ourselves.

As in the US, we made many friends. The Sinclairs invited us to visit their two Collymongle stations in New South Wales, which had 80,000 and 60,000 sheep each. They had 120 dogs but just 20 horsemen, who had to cover enormous distances. At the time a severe drought was severely affecting livestock. I stayed there for three weeks and rode with them, rifle in hand, morning till evening. We shot every sheep we passed. We also shot other pests destroying the crops, including rabbits, wild pigs and emus. The small vegetable plots were surrounded by tall wire fences that reached down for nearly a metre. They deterred some of the animals – although no amount of fencing could keep out the emus. All of this hunting, with wonderful, Savage precision rifles, was essential for preservation. Yet any animals we killed were left on the spot and never eaten.

In 1934, during celebrations for Melbourne's centennial, Italy dispatched its new 5,000-ton cruiser, the *Armando Diaz*. I was 19 and was invited aboard the *Diaz* where, to my joy, I was asked to remain as the captain's guest on a tour of Australia. I was accommodated in the empty hospital area where my cot, a hammock suspended between two poles, swayed and shook in the rolling waves. We reached New Zealand and visited Maori lands. Our group was accompanied by Princess Randi in Maori costume and, as we left, I was granted the honour of rubbing noses with her. We stopped in Wellington, where we attended an official dinner held in the presence of the Duke of Gloucester, the brother of the King of England.

By now it was time to leave the *Diaz* so I reluctantly parted company with her many officers, most of whom were to lose their lives in the coming war. I remember especially a cadet officer from Florence, Alexej Olsoufief who spoke perfect English. He was lost in 1941 during a naval battle. His sister later married Valerio Borghese, a well-known hero in the Italian Navy during the war who led raids in the Mediterranean against the Royal Navy. He sank two British battleships with his miniature submarines in the port of Alexandria.

Back in Australia, I also visited north Queensland with my father and admired the Great Barrier Reef. Aborigines there were friendly towards us, even though we could only communicate in sign language. I was curious to learn how to use the boomerang, and they eventually taught me.

The sea journeys to and especially from Australia were also memorable. These being the days before air transport, I travelled as a passenger on cargo ships. On the return trip, we docked in Perth, Ceylon (now Sri Lanka), along the Malabar coast of India, and at the Suez canal and Alexandria, before arriving in Naples. The whole journey took about 45 days.

One of the most fascinating places was Ceylon. With a few days' stopover, I was able to visit a shrine in Candy, one that attracted great veneration, where a tooth of the Buddha was preserved. We also stopped at Colombo, the capital. During my last visit, sailing back on the *Remo*, I was forbidden to leave the ship. However, I managed to get off with an excuse to see the town centre, only to find that the fakirs and snake charmers had all vanished. An epidemic, probably of cholera, had broken out and many people were taking their dead to be cremated. I quickly returned to the *Remo*.

We also disembarked at Suez and I found passage, together with five Arabs, on an old truck heading for Cairo. The trip cost me one pound sterling and I was not worried by my companions dressed like beggars or by the rickety truck which rattled its way onwards. We met long lines of camels travelling in the opposite direction.

After three hours we arrived in Cairo, and I found the villa of my school friends, the Rossettis. Their mother was a beautiful Greek woman who spoke excellent Italian; their father was the lawyer to King Farouk. The family took me to visit Cairo museum, where all the artifacts of Tutankhamun's tomb, discovered 12 years before, were strewn in various rooms, many of them not yet open to the public. The following day, I returned to the *Remo* for the final crossing to Italy.

In one of these return journeys the ship stopped off in Greece. I briefly visited my mother's first cousin Uncle Lincoln MacVeagh, at the time US ambassador there, and his wife Peggy. But my uncle tried too hard to impress me, claiming he was an expert on all ancient civilisations, Roman, Greek, Etruscan, even Chinese. This arrogance made me uneasy, especially from an American, but I kept my thoughts to myself and politely thanked him before continuing my journey.

Meeting Jessie Owens

I FINISHED MY secondary studies and started to study law at the University of Naples, where I lived with my grandparents. Being a keen sportsman, I presented myself at the pre-trials event for the athletics team, wearing only my tennis shoes. To general amazement I won several races – and the final. The GUF (Gioventu' Universitaria Fascista, or the university fascist youth authority) were so impressed that they gave me a pair of proper trainers for athletics and ordered me to continue training. I decided to take athletics seriously and, to my father's chagrin, left my grandparents to live and train with Ove Andersen, a Finnish finalist in the 3000m steeplechase at the Los Angeles Olympics of 1932.

Figure 3: With my coach, Ove Andersen, in Naples, 1935

Soon after, I was approached by the GUF of the University of Florence. In exchange for me transferring to their institution they promised free books for my studies, no taxes, a job for extra money, and, in particular, the chance to become part of Italy's Olympic athletics team. Of course I accepted, but the authorities in Naples opposed the move.

I was summoned to the office of the head of the Neapolitan GUF and even met the Secretary-General of the National Fascist Party, Achille Starace. They all ordered me to stay where I was. However, I had come to dislike Naples, finding the attitude of many of its inhabitants both servile and pompous, and the political regime at the time held limited cultural appeal. My character and foreign upbringing had nothing in common with the place. I also strongly resented their attempts to order me about. So I to went to Florence and, as punishment, was deprived of my membership of the GUF, but became national university champion and eventually part of the Italian Olympic team. I was delighted with the outcome.

I specialised in the 200m, then the 400m and continued to improve. I won many competitions and, in 1935, I was granted the "Golden M" award, the Littore dello Sport, as sportsman of the year. I received the citation from the Prime Minister, Benito Mussolini.

By 1936 I had become a reserve member of the Olympic team. I was only 21 and had not had enough training under my belt to be in the senior squad. We went to the Berlin Olympics *(original programme, figure 4, right)*, and it proved to be an unforgettable experience. In the Olympic village I met Jessie Owens, of whom we were all in awe. He had won four golds, and what medals: the 100m, the 200m, the long jump and the 400m relay! We became friends as I was one of the few among us who spoke English. I was a witness to his

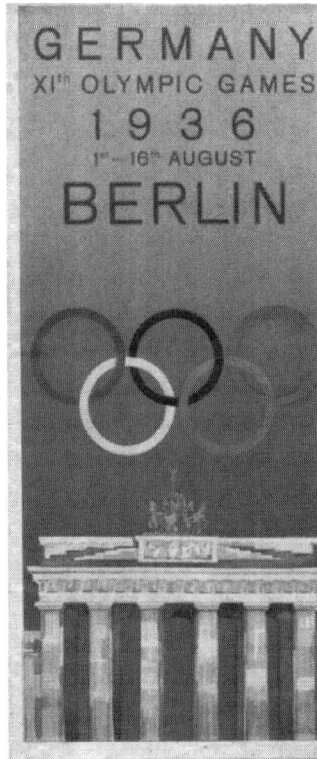

GERMANY
XIᵗʰ OLYMPIC GAMES
1 9 3 6
1ˢᵗ – 16ᵗʰ AUGUST
BERLIN

meeting with Adolf Hitler. Contrary to what was said afterwards, the Fuhrer was quite cordial.

After the Games I took part in other competitions in Italy and abroad, but it all came to an end as war approached.

2: TO WAR

JOINING THE ALPINI

IN MID-JUNE 1937, while I was in Florence, I received my call-up card with orders to leave for the army officers' training course. I suspended my academic studies and my training with the Olympic team and presented myself at the military service station at Bassano del Grappa, in the province of Vicenza, for enrolment in the Corpo degli Alpini (the Alpine corps). I was to remain there, in the mountains, for the next three months.

I was enrolled on a fast-track course for university students to become officer cadets which – so that they could complete their studies – lasted just half the normal six months. I arrived full of enthusiasm and in excellent physical shape – my heart, lungs and muscles were all in perfect condition. I had also benefited from some pre-military discipline, so I knew how to carry a gun, how to command troops in close-order formation, and what it meant to be a soldier.

On my arrival, around forty cadets were present. We were welcomed warmly but with strict discipline. At the initial physical examination, hair that was considered too long was shaved off and our physical fitness was tested. The admission criteria of the Corpo degli Alpini were some of the most stringent in the forces with regard to fitness, but I passed immediately due to my Olympic training. One of my weaker colleagues was turned away and was sent off to join the Bersaglieri corps on another floor of the same barracks.

The cadets were the responsibility of the course commander, Capt Confalonieri, and of Lieut Ghiglione. I later came to know Ghiglione well, but when I first met him he was still the terrible "Lieut Polvere", feared by all for his iron discipline. *Polvere* means dust in Italian. The nickname came from his habit of carrying out regular inspections in white gloves, which he slid over every surface. When any dust was found, a day of punishment or hard labour was immediately inflicted. Capt Confalonieri, on the other hand, maintained the attitude of a superior but rather friendly father figure.

We were quickly issued with our uniforms, an Alpino feathered hat and a corporal's black stripe on our sleeves. This was the first step in our progress towards being officers. The captain explained: "The corporal's stripe is black, but I can assure you, you'll sweat red blood to deserve it! You're here because you are going to become officers and learn how to command others. To do this you will need to learn and to obey orders: if you're university students on the fast-track course we'll expect even more from you. In effect, we assume, even with some reservations, that you are all intelligent people." He said all this, though, with an affable and paternalistic air.

We were issued with our Alpino *zaino* (rucksack). This, we were told, would come to be our dearest friend, our home, our hold-all for everything. However scruffy it might become, we would always want it by our sides. It was much larger than an infantry rucksack. Although we could put anything in it, it had to unfailingly contain a regulation two days' rations and two extra magazines for our model '91 rifles. These items could never be lacking during regular inspections.

Together with the rucksack, we were issued with a "tactical back-pack" which was much smaller and made of coarse grey canvas. This was strapped below the large rucksack and was to be used without the latter in short transfers between military instructions. We were also issued with new hobnailed climbing boots called *scarponcelli* [normal boots] and another heavier pair which were old and second-hand – celebrated amongst the Alpini as trusty *scarponi* [mountain boots]. Both pairs were tied to the knapsack together with a mess tin, a drinking cup and a 1-litre canteen which was larger than normal infantry issue because, as the captain told us, "...you will find yourselves in areas without any water. Your canteens are not just for wine, you know!" He also sarcastically reminded us that we would have to use our *scarponcelli* every day "not only to get blisters on your feet, but also to visit your girlfriends on leave days and to perform gymnastics". We would then have to change to using the proper *scarponi* and, he continued: "These, even if they weigh twice as much" – mine weighed 1.4kg each! – "they will be more comfortable because they're already broken in. You'll wear them on command and love them even more than you love your girlfriends." We were each given a pair of roughly the right size and most of us had considerable problems walking in them – but Confalonieri could not care less.

Bassano del Grappa, north of Vicenza, is known for its position on the slopes of Monte Grappa, made famous from a long series of battles between Austrians and Italians in the First World War. The river Brenta runs through the town, crossed by a historic bridge, the Ponte degli Alpini. The town is also the home of the fiery drink known as grappa.

On our second day, the captain led us in rows of three, with our rucksacks, along the river. He said: "Those with new boots that are too big, go to the left bank and stand in the water; those whose boots are too small, do the same but stand on the right bank. You see, since you're university students, if you stand for ten minutes in the river, there on the right bank, the leather will stretch. But if you stand in the water on the left bank, the leather will shrink ..."

Capt Confalonieri liked to recall the First World War. He once told us: "War is war. It's no joke. Bullets are bullets and dying is nothing. Being wounded is much worse. Being wounded in the stomach is the worst of all because the pain is unbearable." Poor Confaloniere. He died of stomach wounds in 1940, fighting in Albania where he was a division commander. He was decorated with the gold medal for valour, the highest Italian military decoration. He was undoubtedly one of the members of the forces who most deserved it.

The days passed in the barracks with lessons in close-order formation and gymnastics. Maj Bignami showed us how to turn an aerial somersault while fully armed. We often went to the Santa Felicita valley, a few kilometres from Bassano, for shooting practice with our '91 rifles and light and heavy Breda machine guns, or for exercises using hand-grenades. Rock-climbing lessons were occasionally organised at the mountain gymnasium. I was interested in everything, even the generally unpopular, if vital, mule care, which meant looking after our only means of transport at high altitude. Here I learnt to use the horse-brush and curry-comb. I am convinced the animals were grateful for the attention.

After morning inspection by Lieut Polvere, we went down to the mess at around half past six, either by the stairs or by shinning down a rope hung out of the window. In the evenings we were physically drained and went to bed at nine. However, with the approval of Polvere, we might be rewarded with a pass from six until eight-thirty. I nearly always took advantage of this to eat in a trattoria outside the barracks, even though the mess rations were good and more than enough. Everyone's daily rations included a one-kilo loaf of bread.

On the long marches over the mountains, I learnt how to make Vov, a liqueur made from alcohol, sugar, eggs and Marsala wine. With a friend and colleague, Ponti, we sold it at 50 centimes a glass. We always had a bottle in our rucksacks. It only cost us 5 lire a litre to make so we made a tidy profit.

We spent many days marching through the mountains in our hobnailed boots. Our rucksacks weighed up to 35kg and held a blanket and a canvas tent, with a 20-metre manilla rope – for every four soldiers – tied above the rucksack, and boots laced on to the side. Below this we attached our tactical packs.

We immediately appreciated the infinite capacity of our packs. Although they weighed heavily on our shoulders, after a while the burden seemed to disappear even if on our mountain marches we had to walk non-stop for fifty minutes before a ten-minute rest. The days passed and our hobnailed boots became ever more dear to us.

The last march of the course targeted the Asiago high plateau. We set out at 2.30 in the morning and returned at around eight at night. The distance was sixty-two kilometres. We thought it might be impossible to achieve but achieve it we did. We returned to barracks singing one of our Alpino songs.

I finished second in the final cadet classification and, as soon as I was awarded the silver ribbon, which I sewed on to my lapel, I was promoted to the rank of cadet officer. First place on the course went to my friend Levi who was allowed to choose the unit he wanted to serve with in his first position as an officer. He chose the 7th Alpino Regiment, but a few months later I was told he had not been admitted because he was Jewish. I was astounded and disturbed as I asked myself what racism and politics had to do with us. Unfortunately, Fascism obliged us to follow Germany and its regime.

After the course finished, I was called upon directly to act as cadet officer with the 6th Alpino Regiment in Vipiteno, near the Brennero Pass. I solemnly recited the officer's oath: "I swear to be faithful to the king and his royal successors, to obey the laws of the nation for the inseparable good of king and country." I was then ordered to present myself to the Verona battalion, where Maj Gino Gagliotti was commander. In the centre of the town where the regiment had billeted me I left my rucksack and suitcase at the home of the Nones family and returned to the barracks of the Verona battalion. I was cordially welcomed by my new commander.

Figure 5: With my Alpino hat at Metzovo, on the Albanian/Greek front in July 1941

Maj Gagliotti was from Florence like myself and also an Italian military skiing champion. He had been wounded in the First

World War and captured twice by the Austrians, managing to escape from the prison camp. His past had earned him two Bronze Medals for Military Valour. Gagliotti had read my personnel file and, having learnt that I was both a Florentine and an Olympian, asked me to be his chief warrant officer. The Verona consisted of the command company and companies 56, 57 and 58, each led by career officers. The latter had little respect for me as, being only a cadet, I was not deemed equipped to command. However, Gagliotti was keen and continued to tell me: "My dear Lieutenant, with your precedents you'll be a perfect Alpino. I'll show you the real life of the Alpino!"

Gagliotti's subordinate officers had him down as a nutcase, as I came to appreciate myself. I had fallen enthusiastically into my role as chief warrant officer, giving orders to the companies, which was not appreciated by their commanding officers as I lacked the experience of a regular officer with training from the Military Academy. While the Alpini in these companies were called up to take part in exercises, I had to stay in the office with Maj Gagliotti who was most reluctant to be cooped up. One day, he turned round and said: "Lieutenant, you know nothing about skiing. I will have to teach you all about it."

As a result, we spent many days out in the open, well away from the office and where, thanks to the winter snowfall, I learnt to ski. Shortly we were able to ski as far as Bressanone, about 20km away with our two orderlies. Since I was inclined to take on any kind of physical activity, skiing was no problem for me and I met with the major's approval.

In March 1938, the Anschluss took place in Austria when more than 90% of the voting population decided in a referendum to become part of Germany. As a consequence, Italy sent Alpino troops to its eastern borders as it was uncertain if Hitler's sights were also set on the previously Austrian cities of Trento and Trieste. At the same time, Lieut-Gen Rossi, responsible for the entire eastern Alps area, planned the military's Grand Manoeuvres. Maj Gagliotti was ordered to command the Red troops who were to be overcome by the Blue troops.

Maj Gagliotti was completely against this idea. So, one night, the major, accompanied by two Alpino skiers and myself, managed to take prisoner the entire Blue Command, who were camped in the snow in a high mountain cave. The four of us captured them all as they were celebrating something and singing. The manoeuvres were deemed a total failure, they upset all the higher command's plans and Gen Rossi sent a note of reproof to Maj Gagliotti. The latter, however, was delighted at having taken the enemy command prisoner.

In the early months of my appointment, along with my colleagues 2nd Lieuts Pardon and Paride, we started going out with three girls. They were teachers living about 18km north of Vipiteno in the Val Saletto. They called us "the three musketeers" since we were always together and every evening we set out on our bicycles to see them, spend some time with them and return only in the early hours of the morning. My girlfriend was called Lina Pizzarelli. She was from Milan and was a bilingual German teacher who later went to work in Dresden, where my family was also based. She remained on friendly terms with them until after the end of the war.

I continued with the long marches together with Maj Gagliotti. Once, we reached as far as Cima d'Asta, at 3,800m. I elected to carry my own rucksack even if, as an officer, it was supposed to be my orderly who carried it with his own – 60kg in all! But I wanted to be able to understand what the physical state of the Alpini under my command was likely to be. Sometimes, as punishment, I used to order them to follow. They had to come up the mountain behind me, with their heavy rucksacks on their backs, just like me.

While exploring the area on the orders of the Command, I often went up to a depot in the depths of the forest where the munitions were kept, in a glade guarded by German shepherd dogs. The area was cordoned off and the dogs were attached to a metal cable that ran along a wire fence. One day, I found a small wolf pup there which I took back to Vipiteno with me. I remember it was frightened because it had never seen people, cars or houses before. However, the animal slowly got used to being in contact with people even though my colleagues made fun of me and joked that the dog never barked or growled and, even more, it was always frightened. Until, one day, when my orderly was tidying the room in my absence, the dog which had been sleeping permanently under the bed leapt out and bit him on the wrist. From then on, everyone considered it a proper guard dog worthy of respect.

One day, the dog ran away and was later found back at the munitions dump where I had found it. It had crossed two mountain chains to get there despite having spent more than three months with me in the barracks. I brought it back with me but, after a few weeks, it escaped again and so I decided to leave it to its fate as a guard dog of the distant munitions reserve.

Maj Gagliotti and I began the main summer camp manoeuvres and I received orders to set up a rock gymnasium for the Alpini. I was told to set up rock-climbing tests from levels 1 to 4 on the face. I had fun climbing up and down with a double rope, and entertaining the passers-by who gazed up from below and watched me hanging out over the precipice.

THE SPANISH CIVIL WAR

THE INTERNATIONAL SITUATION was worrying for Italy. The League of Nations, founded in 1919 by President Woodrow Wilson of the US, had imposed an embargo on Italy with sanctions that were seriously affecting our economy.

The background for this situation lay in the fact that the Fascist government, intent on emulating other European powers in acquiring its own colonial empire and anxious to prevent the British establishing a protectorate in Abyssinia (modern Ethiopia), invaded and conquered that country in 1936, after a brief war. Italy was roundly condemned, the League declared an embargo and severe economic sanctions were put in place.

Today, in the post-colonial era and with the benefit of hindsight, it is easy to criticise our actions. But, for us at the time, Italy appeared to have as much right as any of the other European nations to acquire overseas territory. National honour demanded that our government should achieve this, if necessary in defiance of active opposition voiced by the other colonial powers. The only European nation not to fall in line with the embargo was Germany, which provided Italy with vital commercial and industrial assistance. This was an odd development, as the Italian people had always found themselves on the opposite side to the Germans, for both geographical and historical reasons. However, this assistance led to the Pact of Steel between both countries and eventually bound them during the world war. The intervention of both countries in the Spanish Civil War also enabled them to start preparing for the wider conflict to come.

In 1936, Spain lurched into civil war. The monarchy had recently been abolished and the new left-wing government had started to impose changes which deeply divided Spanish society. A group of Spanish generals, from among whom Francisco Franco was later to emerge as leader, decided to rebel against the Republican government before these changes became irreversible. They launched a coup but failed to capture the capital, Madrid, while achieving some success in other parts of the country, especially the south. Spain became split between the right-wing Nationalists and the left-wing Republicans. A bloody civil war began.

It cannot be denied that, in leading the rebellion, Franco effectively overthrew Spain's legitimate government, but the causes for this course of action need examining. The coalition of left-wing parties that formed the Spanish Republican government included a well-organised Communist element which aimed to transform the nation into a "popular democracy" on the Russian model. Franco, aware that numerous Spaniards, but also many Western nations, were deeply adverse to Soviet ideology taking root in Europe, acted in accordance with his own ideas of honour and conscience. Past experience of the Russian revolution suggested that the Bolsheviks would not hesitate to seize power by overturning any government in which they participated. Moscow was also taking this unique opportunity to establish a foothold in western Europe, assisting and financing the war against the Nationalists. They were helped and supported in this by volunteers from many nations – the International Brigades.

In 1944, as a POW in Russia, I spoke with some young Spaniards in Lager 27-NKVD. They had been captured by communist units in 1937 in Spain and taken to the USSR to be indoctrinated. After this, they were to be repatriated to Spain to further the Soviet cause.

In February 1939 while I was still with the Verona battalion, we received an order from HQ in Rome for us to form a unit: the Special Alpino Corps. It was planned for overseas duties, and in particular to support Gen Franco's army in Spain. I did not hesitate to volunteer, despite Maj Gagliotti's disappointment. He later admitted that, had he been in my shoes, he would have done the same.

As a result, I was transferred to the Vestone volunteer company (conscripted Alpini with volunteer officers). We all had to wear civilian clothes, without weapons. In the brief time it took to get everything ready, the clothes were all provided new, from berets to shoes. It was amazing to see all of us mountain people in civilian clothing with suitcases in place of rucksacks (everyone, however, hid their precious Alpino hat inside). Like all the officers, I had a few days of leave in which to equip myself with the khaki uniform of Gen Franco's Tercio troops. I was able to get hold of one immediately, from the cap to a beautiful pair of soft brown leather boots. Sewn on to the right sleeve of my shirt was a sparkling white Alpine edelweiss. However, the uniform was hidden in the suitcase. Before leaving Vipiteno, I also devised a secret code so I would be able to avoid postal censorship and write to my schoolteacher girlfriend Lina and thus also to my family.

On a February night we arrived just before dawn at Livorno where, still in darkness, we were hurriedly embarked on a passenger boat. Into the holds were crammed 1,300 members of the company plus our mules (around 150). We secretly set sail for Spain but were overtaken by a great storm the following morning. We were forced to stop over in Palma de Mallorca, where we unloaded the mules which were, by now, dead. Mules die when they get seasick.

Our ship was anchored outside the port and was under the surveillance of two "Non-Intervention" French and English ships. Their crews were amazed to see us unloading all of the animal carcasses on to large rafts. We had orders to remain below deck and many of us became afflicted by the same illness as the mules. The officers, however, were allowed to take a turn on deck and to make fun of the Non-Intervention ships.

We set out again in the evening with a calm sea, heading for Puerto Santa Maria in Cadiz. Here the Alpini were lodged in tents while we officers were welcomed into the homes of private citizens. I was lodging in a beautiful house surrounded by a vast area of land belonging to the owner of a Jerez (sherry) vineyard. The war had left the family with nothing but its wine, and they were all starving. Although I didn't have the time to look after them, I did try to help them as much as I could by getting them bread, cheese, a bit of meat and pasta from our canteen – as did all of my colleagues. Even if the people were not as enthusiastic about Franco as we were, they came to appreciate us – and not just for what we had given them. The locals called us the Cockerels but we were well looked upon, especially by the girls.

Over the next few days, I got to know my new commanding officer, the company commander, Capt Enzo Marchesi, with whom I immediately became friends. As his subordinate platoon commander, he spotted me immediately and advised me to put in a request to become a regular career officer with his support. Capt Marchesi came from the School of War and was a brilliant young officer.[1]

The Special Alpino Corps was forced to stay in Puerto Santa Maria until we had received a new contingent of mules – the Alpini cannot be deployed without them. In the meantime, we continued with tactical manoeuvres to keep the troops fit and in form. It was anticipated that we would participate later in the actions around Madrid where the bloody final battle was being fought.

We were subsequently informed, however, that we would not be used on the front and would soon be returning to Italy. I also quickly became acquainted with the fleas and crabs transmitted by the lovely local girls, as a result of which quite a few of us finished up in hospital. I once covered myself with anti-lice powder made with sulphur. I washed it off with water, forgetting that, on contact with water, the sulphur burns terribly. Particularly on the genitals.

In March 1939 the Civil War was at its climax and much of the population were dying of starvation. We continued to help as much as possible from our own resources. The battle for Madrid ended earlier than expected and the International Brigades ranged against Franco, consisting of French, Belgian, English and Italian Communists under Russian command, were beaten back. Among them was an American division which was annihilated, shamefully, in less than 48 hours.

We received the order to return to Italy without having ever been effectively deployed. The return, in April, took place without incident and we camped near the port where we disembarked at Castellammare di Stabia, near Naples. I had a new companion with me, a puppy called Peseta.

However, the Alpini were by now impatient to return to the Veneto and, as far as they were concerned, Naples was almost worse than Cadiz. What weighed upon them most was the Neapolitan indolence, the lack of concern for others and, above all, the dialect. They found it completely unintelligible. We officers had immense difficulty in restraining our troops, despite firm discipline. After taking over Central Station in Naples and capturing all the horse-drawn carriages in front of it "in the Alpino way", we were at last given the order to depart for Verona, headquarters of the 6th Alpino Regiment. I reached my Verona battalion in Vipiteno on 2nd May. The Special Alpino Corps was disbanded and each unit returned to its own regiment. I found myself discharged but, due to my immediate request to volunteer again, I was taken back into the army and returned to the 6th Regiment.

AN UNTOUCHABLE BLONDE

IN VIPITENO, PESETA the puppy made the acquaintance of our three girls – Lina Pizzarelli and the two girlfriends of Lieuts Pardon and Paride. Once again, the three musketeers were reunited. But our unit was soon transferred to Aosta in north-west Italy and from there we proceeded on foot to Etroubles. We set up our tents along the road to the St Bernardo Pass, in the middle of the winter and under rain that did not let up for three weeks. In this unhappy time we learnt how to make a fire with sodden wood and to sleep in the damp. We were all in a foul mood as we came to realise that this was part of the conscript's lot. I had to leave Peseta with the three girls among the mountain folk of Vipiteno, but along the march a young St Bernard pup started following me and soon became my faithful companion.

Near the village of Castellamonte I found lodgings in the parish governed by the local priest, Don Cipriano, while my platoon and their mules were camped just beyond the church walls. Don Cipriano turned out to be a wonderful character and I soon made friends with both him and his housekeeper. A large man, over two metres tall, he used to wear a filthy black tunic that was dirtied by the snuff he continuously took. He performed baptisms and funerals which were paid for with chickens, geese and eggs. The latter were kept in chalky water in two large barrels at the back entrance to the church. Every evening we ate *bagna cauda* together, a hearty local dish, from a single plate. He drank only half glasses of wine because, he claimed: "The doctor told me that wine is dangerous for my blood pressure. He has forbidden me to drink a single glass of it. So now I only drink half glasses!" The first evening he drank well over 20 of them. I cannot recall the exact number. He frequently pulled from his pocket an enormous piece of cloth, which he called a handkerchief, and blew his nose with a sound louder than the thunder in the Valle d'Aosta. One of his favourite tricks was to do this in church.

In the evening, having checked that everything with the troops was in order, we officers allowed ourselves some time off, leaving those who were on duty to cover our backs. We sometimes went as far as Turin on the train. On one of my outings I went with Lieut Romagnoli in Don Cipriano's priest's clothing. We wandered around near a farm belonging to the family of Gina, a beautiful but unfortunately engaged and therefore (almost) untouchable blonde. After visiting her, I returned to my room at about two in the morning. However, while I was climbing onto the wall of the church courtyard to reach the balcony on the second floor, a shard of glass cut through my shoe. The wound in my foot was deep and left me unable to walk properly for several days.

Around this time, I met up with Sgt Vaona again. He looked after the mules but I had lost touch with him since being in Vipiteno before the Spanish trip. He was from Verona, born in 1908 of illegitimate birth. He had started out in the lowest ranks of the Alpini but had managed to be promoted to the rank of sergeant in charge of the pack animals. This was because, on top of his physical qualities, he had taught himself to read and write. It is rare to find such a friend.[2]

To my great surprise, I was discharged on 5 April 1940 with unlimited leave. I immediately went to Rome, where my father had been transferred from Frankfurt to the Foreign Ministry. There I volunteered for a second time to be in the 6th Alpino Regiment – and was taken back into active service again.

I came into contact with high-level civil servants from the Foreign Ministry and with some of the Fascist hierarchy. My parents had appealed to them to make every effort to avert my being exposed to combat duties.

I was also very close at the time to the family of my cousin Carlo Mottola and, in particular, to his sister Rosanna. Carlo, who also was a personal friend of Italy's Foreign Minister, Galeazzo Ciano[3], was leaving for Albania as the personal secretary to Minister Jacomoni, Lieut-Gen in Tirana.

He was more than happy for me to accompany him. What better a moment than this, it seemed, both to keep me away from danger and, simultaneously, to get me noticed!

However, nothing was further from my mind. I was determined to go to the front with our Alpini. I couldn't care less about the political world and the numerous traps its members laid each other, not just those in the National Fascist Party but also among the diplomats. At the time, a well-known joke went: *armiamoci e partite* (let us take up arms and then (you) go and fight).

In June 1940, I found myself back in Verona. This time I was assigned to the new Val Venosta battalion, preparing for the war against France.

IN PIEDMONT

I JOINED THE BATTALION in Piedmont, north-west Italy, while it was camped along the river Gesso in the vast landholding of the King of Italy. In Valdieri, not far from Cuneo, I met Lucia Grifone, with whom I became intimate friends. During that time I took many photographs, a passion which has remained. I remember her well: a slim, tall blonde in a light blue dress in a field full of flowers before the snow-capped Alps. In the colour photographs, the blue of her dress contrasts strongly with the blood-red poppies.

The war lasted only a few days because France had already laid down arms against Germany. It was later said we Italians had stabbed France in the back but, for us, this was not true at all since, at least in our sector in the Alpes Maritimes, the fighting was harsh and many injuries were taken. Nonetheless, the morale of the French soldiers was low and their artillery was in worse condition than ours – which is saying something.

We found ourselves under an armistice with military operations suspended. I was given charge of the *platone collegamenti* (communications platoon) of the company command. As well as radios and telephones, I had six trained German shepherd dogs and their handlers. I also received twelve cages with homing pigeons. However, they shortly disappeared – "heroically lost in battle" – into our cooking pots.

Among my Alpini, I remember one who was a professional smuggler. He was short and was able to carry a 60kg back-pack (equal to his own body weight) and he was the only one to be awarded a Silver Medal in the field for his conduct at the front. He was often absent at evening roll-call and was regularly punished, but he managed to avoid sanctions since, at four in the morning, despite being completely drunk, he was always at his station. He did his duty and that was all I wanted – this is the true meaning of being an Alpino.

When we crossed the border with France through the Col delle Finestre at the end of June, we descended to S. Martin Vesubie. There I met some people who could still remember the Marquis de Ruffano, my grandfather. From 1897 to 1901, he had passed the summers there with my family together with Alfonso Borbone of the Two Sicilies, Count of Caserta, titular heir to the Kingdom of Naples.

While entering French territory, many men were found to be afflicted by gout from the water. As a result, we were obliged to add a lot of iodine to the morning coffee – it was disgusting. Horse flies also infested us and the dog section suffered the most, so much so that we had to send them back to their training centre in Trieste with their handlers. I was then detached from the platoon with sixteen Alpini and sent to Punta Baus de la Frema, at 2250m altitude, on the demarcation line established by the Armistice. This was further inside French territory, and our job was to signal any eventual enemy movements.

Baus de la Frema was an inaccessible peak and we set up our camp just below the summit. Below us a pasture was covered with edelweiss. Since we had a weak radio and a heliograph that worked only in sunshine, we often could only communicate with the battalion with signal flags. Since I was particularly fit at the time, I went down with a couple of Alpini every day to pick up the rations, the wine and water. I personally took up the wine barrel because, otherwise, it would have arrived only half full. Below us we could see the small amount of traffic on the road that wound tortuously from Col S. Martin down to the village of Besançon. However, my attention was often concentrated on the formidable Conchetas Fort. This was built on a rocky promontory above Besançon on Le Conquette peak at 1,670m. Its eastern flank faced Italy, ranging across Val Vesubie and Boreone. With binoculars I could see camouflaged gun-emplacement slits in the rock face. I paid particular attention to the French flag which fluttered over the fort, day and night.

I wanted to know why the flag remained up at night. So I thought up a plan with my men to find out. Obviously, any belligerent action during the armistice was out of the question since it would be considered a criminal act. However, between the two armistice lines the ground was legally neutral. So I chose a volunteer and, one afternoon, I dropped down into the valley with him, unarmed and in cobbled-together civilian clothes: a jacket turned inside out and trousers worn as plus-fours. We looked like peasants on a day out. We took our chance.

We had no problems descending and could see no-one near the north-eastern side of the fort. We were sitting on a low wall, looking towards Besançon, when we suddenly realised a French soldier was close by. He was watching us from behind. Calmly, I offered him a cigarette. He refused and went on his way. Perhaps he was taken in by our guise as two simple peasants. I had spoken to my companion in a halting French that he did not appear to understand.

When we returned to base, I continued to think about the fort. I was wondering were there *any* soldiers inside? I had an idea that it would be worth trying out a reconnaissance. But what would happen if we were found out?

A FLAG FROM FORT CONCHETAS

ON THE BASIS OF the recce we had made a few days earlier around the fort, I chose a dark night with a cloudy sky to get to the rock itself. Seen so many times through my binoculars, it appeared to be a large fort dug out of the rock face.

One of my Alpini, Cpl Sante, volunteered to accompany me. Armed only with bayonet, rucksack and pocket torch each, we descended southwards from Baus de la Frema, slowly getting used to seeing in the dark. It was mid-August and the cloudy sky was perfect for the operation. After leaving our rucksacks on the edge of the wood at the bottom of the Vallon de Vernet, we carefully reached the open space in front of the fort. I feared it might be mined. We went round it and passed under a wire fence with watch-towers. The fence might have been electrified but we managed not to touch the wires. We passed over a small trench and, still undisturbed, began to climb the rockface that led to the Italian aspect of the fort. Ascending steadily, we soon reached the top, and entered the defenceworks through a large concrete slit. It was the mouth of a gun emplacement.

Inside, a steel well descended vertically. We remained still on the slit for a few long moments as the footsteps of a look-out sounded just above our heads. In our total darkness Sante was becoming agitated, so I had to calm him down. Then, bayonet in hand, I crept back out from the emplacement. We could not afford to be captured. We would eliminate the lookout if we had to. But the footsteps had stopped by now so I returned through the slit. While I had been out, my companion had become so afraid that he had shit himself. The stench was terrible. He had to get rid of his underpants.

We both dropped down the well and, by the light of our torches, got into the fort. It passed through my mind that, without recognising who I was, Sante might kill me in the dark. In time though our confidence increased. We decided to carry out a detailed examination of the fort having quickly realized that it had a panoramic view of the Italian border. We measured at 125m the length of an underground corridor that led from the main entrance straight to the barred door. A second corridor ran straight for 55 metres. We also managed to count the number of steps that led down to the wells, thereby calculating the height. But my main interest, the real reason for being here, was the flag we could always see flying from Baus de la Frema. Our last inspection was of a shed outside the command post, and from this we realised that it would be impossible to lower the flag on a pulley. The flagpole was just a pine trunk and the rope that held it up had snagged against the stump of a branch. And now, the fear that had initially gripped us – that the guard might have spotted us and gone for reinforcements – returned stronger than ever. What could we do now that we were inside? There was no way back.

I could read indecisiveness in Cpl Sante's eyes.

"Come on," I said, "it's all or nothing. I'll go up and get the flag and you stay here as look-out."

From a concrete platform I managed to climb up the tree, supported by the stumps of branches that had been sawn off. I reached the top, grabbed the flag and pulled it down along with its rope.

"Ours at last," I thought to myself.

Quickly, we returned to the corridor, and retraced the same route to the gun-emplacement that we had entered before dropping down the rockface. By now we had booty. We took with us a wooden first-aid box, painted white with a French flag, a heavy Hochkiss gun-barrel, several delicious stock cubes for my colleagues at the observatory, a marble compass slab, documents from the fort and the shed and, above all, the flag which was securely inside my shirt. Taking great care not to be seen, or to touch the barbed wire or trip on possible mines, we finally returned to our rucksacks. Heavily loaded up, at dawn we slowly climbed back up to Baus de la Frema. We arrived unscathed – except for my colleague's pair of underpants that we had exchanged for the flag.

The euphoria of this successful night raid was increased by being able to offer to Command some detailed information not only about Conchetas Fort but also about the main defensive and offensive works along the Alpine sector. When I sent my detailed report on the fort in 1940, I wrote in the accompanying letter: "I have received these documents from two Italians residing in the area and who are naturalised French. The sketches I have made and the details contained are the result of the information received." Unfortunately, the Alpini talked and what really happened soon became known to all. For this reason, all the details about the fort, with the related diagrams, were sent back to me. The authorities kept only the main documents on connections with other forts in the area, the methods of command contacts and the compass slab which pinpointed military sites and fortifications. The latter was made of marble, 24cm in diameter and 4cm thick. Although broken, it had been very heavy to carry in a backpack up to 2000 metres.

The documents returned from Command were accompanied with a note: "As we are in an armistice period, the officer responsible for this action could be subject to the maximum punishment with demotion. If we had been in war, he would be awarded the highest medal. Since nothing has emerged on the part of the French, it is preferable to return to him the French flag taken, together with the documents relating to the raid. He should be severely warned."

I admit that I effectively placed Higher Command in a precarious position. During an armistice, where the two parties must suspend all activities for a set period, taking the flag from an enemy fort together with their plans and documents was both illegal and inexcusable. "So, not a word should be said about it. And the person participating should keep the flag for himself, hoping that nothing comes to light," they concluded. [4]

A NAKED SKIING TRIP

AT THE END OF AUGUST 1940, our battalion was ordered to leave the western front and we crossed back into Italy. That same autumn, I received the order to take a selected group of 35 to 40 Alpini for a 10-day skiing trip for training in the high Alps.

The Alpini are elite troops who specialise in mountain or Arctic warfare. Then, as now, they were proficient rock climbers and skiers. My orders were to ensure this group of advanced skiers continued their intensive training and were kept in top physical shape. But why choose me? I had received some training in skiing, but my knowledge and experience at the time were far from making me the ideal choice for a unit of chosen specialists. Only later did I realise that my personal file must have mentioned my athletics training as a member of the Olympic team. In addition, my previous CO and skiing instructor, Maj Gagliotti, himself a former skiing champion, was likely to have provided a positive – if not optimistic – evaluation of my abilities.

Travelling on two buses, we left the town of Domodossola, near the Swiss border, and reached Val Formazza, where we camped at 2,000m in small barracks, surrounded by immaculate snow. We were not far from a ski resort and a large hotel, which had few customers at that time of the year. They were delighted to serve us *grappa* in the evenings.

Despite being conscious of my limited ability in skiing, I gave it all I could ... and this was not lost on the men. The weather stayed clear, no wind blew and the temperature was sub-zero. The 10-day training period went quickly.

I wanted to end our stay on a high note so, two days before leaving, I liaised with the hotel and made a satisfactory agreement with them. After a skiing excursion in the nude, our group would appear around midnight in the hotel lounge, to drink two bottles of *grappa* graciously offered by the management. We would be naked except for our ski boots and our briefs, "to hide our balls to the public". Everyone was excited. What better publicity for the hotel? And for us, something never done before.

When I put this to my Alpini, the feelings were mixed at first. They had never done anything like it. When one of them with a cold and a slight fever expressed his doubts, I replied: "Don't worry, there is no better remedy for your cold." I added that I would be with them all the way, as always.

Our platoon assembled at night, as planned, in only our ski boots and briefs. We shouldered our military-issue skis and started climbing to the top of the hill. Despite the freezing temperature, we performed the climb and the descent, twice. It all went without a hitch. We arrived at the hotel lobby just after midnight, to the general enthusiasm of the hotel staff and their guests. After drinking our *grappa*, we descended to our barracks. It had been a great success.

Our nocturnal excursion became instant news in the area, raising comments everywhere, except from the military authorities. They preferred to keep silent and pretend it had never happened.

3: ALBANIA

ITALY GOES TO WAR

O N 23 SEPTEMBER 1940, the Vice-Chief of Staff, Gen Ubaldo Soddu, announced a partial demobilisation of the army. This followed a series of orders and counter-orders, by which units were placed on permanent leave only to be recalled days later. To appreciate the significance of all this, it is necessary to understand the military situation in Italy at the time. (After the war, it emerged that this had been absurd.) By mid-1940, Mussolini intended to join the war alongside Germany, but the question remained of where and when. At the time, Germany appeared to be unstoppable. The Wehrmacht had occupied Poland, France, Belgium, the Netherlands, Denmark and Norway. The United Kingdom had been forced to abandon the continent, Spain was neutral but benevolent, Austria had voted to become part of Germany, America was firmly isolationist and the Soviet Union was Germany's ally.

Furthermore, Germany was fast gaining influence in central Europe and had just secured Romania's support, and supplies from its oilfields. The war seemed all but over and Mussolini wanted Italy to take advantage of any settlement determining the boundaries of the new Europe. He also felt ashamed to have let Germany win the war on its own and was looking for an opportunity to intervene.

Although aware that Italy was not yet prepared to sustain a long period of hostilities, Mussolini had been influenced by the servile and misleading information provided by his General Staff and ministers (and, in particular, Ciano, the Minister for Foreign Affairs). They assured him that a short military operation against Greece would involve a relatively small number of units at little risk, enabling Italy to sit at the winners' table. It would be nothing more than a "stroll in the park". Mussolini received assurances that the Greek army was demoralised, that the mountainous region rear the Albanian border would effectively prevent effective defence by the Greeks, and that the population would welcome the Italian troops. In addition, the occupation of Greece would limit the range of the Royal Navy and help preparations for moving against Suez[5].

After repeated hesitations, the Duce fell for this idea. But he became so confident that, instead of continuing military preparations, he decreed a partial demobilisation, affecting all those born in 1914 and 1915. This was also aimed at releasing manpower for the harvest but, in practice, it deprived us of many trained units. The Julia division of the Corpo degli Alpini was sent ahead on its own, crossing the border between Albania and Greece on 1st October 1940. They were in their summer uniforms, had no heavy artillery and had limited supplies. The demobilisation was not reversed until the end of November, when the Greek campaign had already started with disastrous consequences for our armed forces.

I made my third request to volunteer, this time for the Albanian front. As I was waiting, I took the occasion to pass a few days with my girlfriend Lucia and her family at Carmagnola. We considered ourselves as engaged, despite the reluctance of my parents. They were concerned that her father was a modest municipal secretary. I couldn't care less.

Since I was 10 years old I had been separated from my family while my father was a diplomat in America and I was alone at boarding school in Rome. I had suffered terribly because adolescence is when a son most needs his parents' affection. By now I was 26 and considered myself to be independent. All my future war correspondence was sent to Lucia and to my Aunt Emma de La Feld in Rome. She was my father's younger sister and thought of me as a son, despite the fact that my father had tried many times to discourage me from keeping in touch with her due to long-standing family disputes.

In the last months of 1940 I also went to Naples to visit my grandparents. From there, in civvies together with Don Visendaz, the chaplain of the former Val Venosta battalion, I went to Bari where the troops were departing for Albania. Despite the lack of official news, it could be intuited within the military environment that the fighting in Albania was hard. I was convinced that I would be sent there shortly. I did everything possible to get personal supplies in Rome and Florence of everything that I might need for the front, taking into account that the winter season was nearly upon us.

The call-up card arrived in December 1940. The Tappa Command in Bari ordered me to wait but to contact them twice a day and not to leave the city. The days passed with nothing to do. I met another Alpino lieutenant, also a volunteer, Augusto Platone, whom I immediately befriended. I saw many other soldiers leaving but the situation was horrible. Every hotel was full but I managed to find lodgings. The famous Neapolitan actor Totò was appearing at the theatre to the great enthusiasm of the crowds. I was unimpressed by the act and the actor but, with my new binoculars, I was able to examine in close up the show's troupe of beautiful dancing girls.

DEPARTURE FOR ALBANIA

ON 16 JANUARY, I had my first encounter with the *Galilea*. I embarked on it with my friend Platone and we headed for Albania. With ominous rumours on our situation in Albania circulating all around, I wrote to my Aunt Emma: "In memory of all the kindnesses received, I will write every now and again from the front and, if I should pass on to the other world, I will come to you at night wearing a white sheet and an Alpino hat with a black feather." It was raining and the sea was calm. We arrived in Durazzo (Durres) on 17th January 1941 and went on to Tirana, the capital, by truck. My friend Platone was immediately assigned to the Julia division while I was sent to the Pusteria. Although we were separated, we were still only a few kilometres apart on the same front. We met up again a few weeks later in the Gemona battalion of the 8th Alpino regiment, Julia division. He had the rank of 1st Lieut while I, being younger, was still a 2nd Lieut.

During the few hours of rest in Tirana, in the hostel of the Tappa Command and at the officers' mess, I quickly realised that our military situation was disastrous. On average, each Italian was fighting against seven or eight Greeks, supported by British troops and French mortars. The "stroll in the park" much vaunted by our government could not have been further from the truth. Our Alpini of the Julia had been equipped with little Italian flags to hand out to a welcoming population when they crossed the frontier on 28 October 1940. However, the welcome they received was of machine gun and mortar fire. Furthermore, our surviving soldiers were still wearing summer clothes, with rough canvas uniforms and short capes. They had no blankets, and food and munitions were in crisis because the road network for supplies was virtually non-existent. The weather was unusually frigid with interminable rain, cold and frost. Clayey mud was everywhere. After only three months of war, the enemy had bled our troops and they were riddled with dysentery and frostbite. They had been forced to retreat almost to Berati, back across the Albanian border.

And what about the air force? In such conditions, we could at least expect air-drops. However, as soon as our planes arrived over the lines to deliver munitions and food, they were followed within minutes by the Royal Air Force, who destroyed what the Italians had dropped. It seemed as if they were in it together. Sometimes our own planes machine-gunned us, possibly unable to distinguish us from the Greeks from the air. This situation has always been a great mystery for me, leaving a number of large question marks.

On the morning of 19 January in Tirana, before leaving for the front, a soldier who had left hospital after convalescing from a wounded leg advised me to get myself some leather leggings. He said: "they're the best thing for saving your feet. You don't know what the mud is like here." I didn't lose any time in finding a pair of leather leggings that went from the ankle up to my knees, tied with gut laces. I am certain this advice saved my life.

On leaving Italy I thought I was equipped with everything needed for the campaign. Physically speaking, I was in perfect form. Unfortunately, only those on a front can be fully aware of what is needed although my experience on the Spanish and French fronts was undoubtedly useful. Apart from the usual wooden military box with a change of clothes that could be transferred to new divisional commands, I loaded my heavy rucksack on to my shoulders with everything I thought would be useful. I also had my Leica camera, a large pair of binoculars and a plastic envelope for papers around my neck. On my belt was a large jack-knife which became a dagger when opened. I was confident of being safe in every possible circumstance. Nobody supplied me with a helmet and, as far as I was concerned, I preferred my Alpino hat. It was lighter and less bulky. I felt that the helmet could only protect my head while leaving the rest of my body exposed to every possible fatal wound. A helmet would be like an umbrella, which only the English find useful to protect themselves from the rain. Like ostriches that bury their heads in the sand.

UP TO THE FRONT LINE

ON 19 JANUARY IT WAS RAINING in Tirana before I was taken southwards in a truck with a group of Alpini. I had already seen my friend Platone leave before me. After more than two hours on the pot-holed highway, near Berati we reached a dirty and dilapidated house, where I found command HQ. We arrived shortly after a British bombardment which killed and wounded many. A Sicilian lieutenant-colonel, Eugenio Canino, welcomed me warmly on hearing that his brother had been my captain in the Val Venosta battalion. He had a small mess tin with coffee brought to me by the guard, saying: "You know, this is very rare, only for special moments."

He continued by reading me an express telegram which had just arrived from supreme command in Tirana: "Inform 2nd Lieut Ferrante di Ruffano assigned to your unit, to transfer himself returning to Tirana to this supreme command, signed Visconti Prasca, Supreme Commander of the Armed Forces in Albania." I quickly realised that this was the work of my cousin Carlo Mottola, who was now the lieutenant-general's assistant in Tirana, and who wanted to keep me away from the front.

"No, *Signor Colonnello*, I'm a volunteer so I'm going to the front and I'm staying there. All those soldiers in Tirana enjoying the war making heroic statements while sipping an espresso, in impeccable uniforms with shiny boots and a whip, could I be like them? Never!" I apologised for my frankness and Lieut-Col Canino invited me to give my parents his name: "You never know. If something happens to you, they can ask me here at 4th Army Corps Command since I now am your friend." I replied that it would be he who would eventually inform my parents of my death and not the other way round.

After spending a damp night in a haystack under non-stop rain, about a dozen of us headed into the mountains a few hours before dawn and began the long march south. We had three mules loaded down with bread and munitions. We were destined for the Trento battalion of the 11th Alpino regiment. I had orders to present myself to Maj Zorio, its commander, who was holding the front at Monastir Codra.

*Figure 6: Alpini and their mules in the Albanian mud,
February 1941*

"Is this for the entire battalion?" I asked, considering that it had more than a thousand men.

"Yes, the battalion has been decimated. Besides, this is all we have to give them."

The instructions from Command were precise in another way: "You have to know that there are still Albanians in the area. We have orders to kill them all because they have gone over to the enemy. Everyone, without exception. Remember."

Thinking that there would be a great lack of food, I took a large loaf for myself. The march became ever more difficult, long and tiring. The dawn gave way to rain and sleet along ground of red-clay mud. Wherever we went, we ended up knee deep. "Thank goodness I got those shin pads," I thought to myself. We climbed ever higher. Orienting myself on the map, I tried to establish where I was. A bearded Alpino informed me that life here was a living hell for everyone.

"Bloody war, *Signor Tenente*! The poor sods up at the front are dying like flies. See this mule? Now it's carrying bread but, if it ever gets up there, with the Greek mortars and all this mud, it will be coming down loaded with frozen, wounded men, loaded up like sacks. And these poor beasts are dying too because of those

English planes that machine-gun and bomb us. God damn it! Our own planes drop us food and munitions and then turn and run, and the enemy planes destroy it all. And the Greeks, all around us, they keep coming forward. For Christ's sake. You'll see what a mess it all is."

Along the uphill path we stopped a moment to catch our breath and a wounded soldier appeared. He was being brought down on a stretcher by two Alpini. It was an officer and distressing for me to recognise Lieut Gabigiosu who had been with me at the Verona battalion in 1938. By now he was a captain and a bullet had penetrated one of his lungs. He could only just whisper, but he recognised me.

"Why are you here?" he murmured.

I replied that, after being dismissed, I had volunteered and I was going to the Trento battalion.

"Stupid idiot," he whispered and the stretcher set off again.

At moments like this, on a path taking me to the front, I would have expected at least one word of encouragement from a regular officer and a friend. A "well done, you're doing the right thing" rather than a "stupid idiot".

We continued laboriously through the mud, the rain and the sleet towards our destination. The Alpini only had short capes which reached to just above the knee and they were soaking wet. Still, despite these summer uniforms, they could at least cover themselves with the tent canvas.

We continued towards Treviri and Monastir Codra for our meeting with the Trento battalion – if it was still there. Soon we could clearly hear artillery shots as they came ever closer. Finally, on the top of a bare and rocky mountain, I presented myself to the commander of the battalion, Maj Zorio. Covered by his balaclava he turned out to be cordial, almost paternal in manner. Under camouflaged canvas, seven or eight filthy officers were covered in mud, unshaven and, above all, very tired. Maj Zorio had a helmet with a hole in its side brought to me: "You'll need it," he said. "It's from someone who died this afternoon."

"This evening," he continued, "you'll be going up to the division just over the crest. There aren't many of us left now. All we've got left is some coffee and biscuits. There is no food since no-one can reach us here. However, a nice glass of *grappa* will do you good."

FIRST BATTLES

THAT NIGHT IT stopped raining. On the peaks all around, we could begin to see blotches of black in the white of the snow, where mortar and artillery shells had landed. Together with an Alpino, I travelled along the crest to reach the dip of Chiaf-El-Sofiut. The enemy was not far off on the other side. About twenty men were hidden among the shrubs and rocks.

At dawn, the enemy began firing on us with mortars and machine-guns. Our men, who were hidden, fired off small 45mm mortars and machine-guns as soon as a khaki uniform of the Greek army appeared on the horizon. Protected by my rucksack which I hoped would be mistaken for a rock, I fired off several rounds from my rifle. I had always been an excellent shot and with the enemy at only 200 to 300 metres, I couldn't miss.

Suddenly, the rate of fire from the enemy guns increased. The "ta-tatata, ta-tatata, ta-tatata" of the Greek trumpets indicated an assault, and we were forced to retreat.

"We cannot leave all these munitions on the ground," I told myself. I lifted a box of machine-gun rounds but had to drop it as soon as I saw a fallen Alpino nearby. He had been hit in the leg, and was groaning. I loaded him on to my shoulders and we managed to withdraw behind the crest where, in a sea of mud, more of our men lay. I took one of the dead men's jackets and with this and two rifles, I put together a stretcher and the other Alpini helped me to transport the wounded man to cover. I never knew his name but at least I had got him to safety and had shown the others how to improvise a stretcher. How could you leave a colleague who calls out: "*Tenente*, don't leave me!"

I found myself back at my battalion which was, by now, down to around one tenth of its original size with just 120 men. Below us was a sea of slippery mud and I noticed an unlucky mule that had sunk up to its belly in the slime. Several Alpini were trying to pull it out. I imagined not much more could be done for the beast, but it would at least provide us with some meat since we were all suffering from terrible hunger. The enemy was advancing and their mortars and artillery bombarded us without respite, but we had to hold this position at all costs. There was no trace of our air force to be seen.

I found myself on a small raised area with the Greeks below us, and attacking. Two Alpini were carrying a box of OTO hand grenades. They were the only munitions left to us. I frantically opened the box so I could hand them out but found only heavy stones inside! No grenades at all. Now even Italy was working against us. Damn them all! So we were forced to retreat once more. We still had our bayonets and I had some grenades in my pockets. "Come on, boys," I shouted, "we're alone here, but let's get them anyway!"

Surprisingly, the enemy began to retreat and their firing moved to our right. This was possibly due to the setting of the sun but also due to the large number of losses they suffered. Then when we, encouraged, were ready to counter-attack with our bayonets and our few munitions left, an Italian officer came running towards us. He had a red tie on, his uniform was still clean and he had no weapons. He belonged to the Lupi di Toscana division, the infantry force sent to support us.

I shouted at him: "But, you're unarmed! Not even a gun or a pistol?"

"Run, run," he cried, "the Greeks are here!"

Without thinking about it, I pulled out my pistol to shoot him.

"Coward!" I yelled. But despite my disgust I didn't shoot, in the hope that others would carry it out for me. "Go back and get yourself a weapon. You're not coming through here or you'll be shot." On hearing this, the officer disappeared. Our attack was suspended and now we had to look after the wounded. I wondered how it was possible that the infantry, which had come to reinforce us, could run away at the first sight of the enemy.

I saw one of my Alpini who had fallen. Blood was running from a gaping wound in his chest. He was dead and I left him there. I forgot to take his dog tag.

I was tormented by great doubts but, nonetheless, I was forming a good experience of what war was all about, especially the use of mortars. It was well known that among all the arms in use in this last great war, the mortar was the most lethal, the most precise and the easiest to manoeuvre. From where we were situated then, if I heard an acute long whistle, then this meant that the bomb had a fairly tight trajectory and that the blow would fall on the mass of snow to my left. If the whistle was deeper and decreasing, then the trajectory was more curved and it would fall a few hundred metres away. However, if, instead of a whistle, I heard a short growl like an angry cat, then the bomb was going to fall a few metres away and it was preferable to get our heads down. "Good hit, damn them!" I would whisper as the shrapnel tore through the air and the bits I picked from my back-pack were still burning hot as I threw them away.

Figure 7: An Alpino corpse lies beside a Greek after hand-to-hand fighting on Mount Golico, 24 March 1941

We weren't there to have fun and, in fact, we were playing with our lives. From the prisoners we captured, among them two British officers, we learned that the enemy, aware we were exhausted, had received considerable reinforcements. Three divisions would be putting pressure on the entire area.

The Julia division had been bled dry and was called back to reform itself after a brief rest period. It was situated a few kilometres south of us and had been the first to cause some serious problems to the enemy, fighting on whatever the cost. But we in the Pusteria were also in poor shape. Our numbers had been greatly reduced and we had no food or munitions. Our reinforcements, infantry and Black Shirts, arrived to assist us but ran away immediately, leaving us in the lurch. The enemy dominated us with its 82mm French mortars against our 45mm and 81mm ones. And, even if we captured some of their munitions, we couldn't use them. Everything seemed to conspire to demoralise us. Nonetheless, we were united by team spirit.

As each day passed, we realised more and more how tragic our situation was. But what demoralised us was not the Greek mortars, nor the cold, the rain and the mud, not even the hunger, but the suspicion in the back of all our minds that the war was being played out behind our backs. Despite all the dead, wounded and victims of frostbite, we could find no resentment against the Greeks, only an unpleasant feeling that we were fighting an enemy simply defending its own home. The doubt crept into my mind, then turned into a certainty, that it was we who were in the wrong. I am convinced that every soldier, of whatever rank or position, was of the same opinion. Our hatred was concentrated on the British and the French, who had nothing to do with things here and who were supporting the Greeks.

In the few hours at my disposal, I slept leaning against my back-pack under any form of protection I could find. I was constantly tormented by the lice which calmed down in the cold but which revived as soon as there was a minimum of warmth. I found a moment to write to my Aunt Emma. I sent her my last will since there was no certainty that I would come out of this alive.

ON RECONNAISSANCE

ONE EVENING, I received an order to leave at dawn with three men to reconnoitre an area towards the south-east, as we were shortly to be on the move towards the severe fighting taking place on Mali Trepelit. I was picked because, having arrived more recently, I was less fatigued. Armed with our '91 rifles and hand-grenades, we proceeded without obstacle, when, coming down into a little valley, I saw a dilapidated house with a wisp of smoke wafting from the chimney.

I remembered the words of Lieut-Col Canino: "If you find any Albanians in the area, eliminate them all. They are on the side of the enemy."

*Figure 8: A machine-gun emplacement after
a cold night in Albania, February 1941*

We approached the little house with extreme caution. One Alpino was with me, the other two went round the back. My hand-grenades were ready, bayonet in one hand, pistol in the other. The door was ajar. I threw it open and saw an old woman holding a baby sitting near the fire. She was petrified. No-one was behind the door, or in the room. She was alone with the baby. I raised my arm to reassure her. From what I gathered, her son, the father of the baby, was away. The Alpino behind me was shaken, but remained ready. I drew closer and patted the baby's cheek. He was crying and so was his grandmother. I wanted to help so much, but I had nothing to give them. So we left the house. With a whistle I called back the other two and we went on our way. I would never have been capable of killing the old woman and the baby and, even if the father had appeared, how would I carry out the command? I was at peace with my conscience. Outside the house we found a sack full of corn, the food of the Albanians. I filled my pockets. We were hungry too.

In order to report that we had found nothing, I left my rucksack with one of my three Alpini. They were to continue along the footpath, leaving me free to take a short-cut straight to the top where our unit was situated. At the same time, shelling by artillery and mortars resumed. It reminded me of the summer of 1938, when I was training in Val di Fassa under Maj Gagliotti. On the orders of the major, I was heading straight down the mountain with a message for the unit below who were firing their machine-guns. Their fire suddenly hit the hill I was descending and I continued running down, jumping from rock to rock, trying to dodge ricochets. On my arrival, I was greeted by an astonished Capt Dona' who said: "We thought we had seen a chamois (wild goat), but it was you. You're mad!"

Now, the firing was in earnest.

On reaching the Trento battalion, I learned that the Alpino with whom I had left my rucksack had vanished. I felt naked, without clothing, equipment, cagoule, toilet paper or camera. "*Porca naja!*" I thought[6]. Maj Zorio gave me the rucksack of one of our dead, but it was light and practically empty.

The RAF continued to strafe the area and to bomb the food supplies and ammunition parachuted down by our own planes. As always, they immediately turned tail and fled. Luckily we were no longer directly bombed. From the air perhaps it was difficult to distinguish between the grey-green of our troops and the Greeks' khaki. In the snow of this blasted country they appeared identical.

Whenever and wherever we could, we would fall asleep, at times with sub-zero temperatures. We registered many cases of frostbite to hands and feet. When we could find any, we ate crackers and when possible we lit small fires behind rocks, melted some snow in our mess tins and drank a few mouthfuls of hot water. Sometimes, I took corn seeds from my pocket and placed them on a flat stone heated by the fire. The corn popped and I made pop-corn the American way, an unknown custom in Italy at the time. Our air force, unable to drop any food for us on the front line, was, however, successful in dropping carobs for our mules. We took the carobs, crushed them and with melted snow made them into a sort of porridge which we could not call soup but, with the condiment of hunger, was not too bad after all.

But it was hardly possible, despite our efforts, to continue fighting with so little food or to go without rest for days and nights. The only satisfaction for us was lying in wait for the enemy. Our old '91 rifles, despite rain, wind, cold and snow, never failed us and worked without a hitch. "Here is my pill, friend, and go to hell!" Sometimes we went to the assault with only our bayonets and, even though few in numbers, we managed to get the enemy to pull back. In hearing our battle-cry "Savoia!" the enemy retreated and we felt more encouraged. Lice, our dear friends that had started to visit us during the Spanish Civil War, returned with enthusiasm and gave me no peace (always better than crabs, I philosophised). They multiplied themselves in the lining of my woollen shirt and trousers.

I would like to mention the problem of lice, for the readers who have yet to experience their kind attentions. These insects try their hardest to show their affection by staying so very close to you. Their appearance can be grey, dark with a cross on their backs, or cream if they are young. They prick you delicately and travel all over you, causing you to itch. You try to scratch but cannot find them. They smell and leave their eggs in the most inaccessible places, usually in the seams of any type of clothing, preferably wool; even when the clothes are washed in boiling water the eggs generally survive. Lice will leave a body only when it is cold and dead and will immediately try to locate another host. All war veterans know them, having tried to find them, with infinite patience or boiling rage. They crush them between their fingernails.

Demoralised as we were about the lack of everything, we cursed the lack of supplies and the unit commands who ignored the front-line soldier, the only one giving his life for his fatherland. And what was our concept of fatherland? For us, it was a pig-headed notion that, where we stood, the enemy would not pass, come hell or high water. In any case, we had received the order to defend our positions to the last man. An order issued personally by Mussolini. To hell with him too!

STRUCK BY ILLNESS

IN THE MEANTIME I was suffering from diarrhoea, which forced me to go to the toilet several times in an hour and started to sap my energy. However, I tried to keep my spirit stable, and was almost at peace in being there. I now accepted that death was one of the possibilities of my situation. I had no use for the helmet and I left it on a stick near a badly wounded Alpino, in the hope that he would be found, alive or not. I still had my cagoule and my Alpino hat with the eagle's feather. Maj Zorio had just been promoted to Lieut-Col, even though he had yet to receive the stripes. He appeared filthy, lice-ridden like me, with a long beard. His battalion was shrinking by every passing day. The increasing number of frostbite victims, some with early gangrene, still lacked medical care. They could only be helped with crude bandages.

On the morning of 6th February 1941, the enemy moved into the area around Dobruscia and Mali Spandarit, but their attack was contained. The major and I made huge efforts to avoid being hit by rifle and mortar fire. That same morning I received the order to transfer to another unit. The major didn't like the idea, but said: "My dear friend, you have been transferred to the Julia division; it looks like all the remaining officers are needed to reconstitute it. You should first go to hospital though, because of that diarrhoea and receive some medical attention. You leave tomorrow morning with the patrol." I was really sorry to leave these Alpini; but to go to the Julia, where I had hoped to be destined from the beginning and to find my friend Platone, was a great joy. "Yes, Sir," I said.

As it happened, I stayed with the Pusteria for another two days as only six officers remained of the 25 that had started the campaign and, helped by dense fog, Greek patrols had become more active.

Just before dawn on 8 February I left with the patrol. We had two mules loaded with injured men, mostly with severe frostbite, and headed to our hospital near Mali Trepelit. At the same time a small contingent of reinforcements arrived, many after being released from the same hospital. About twenty men in all, they were still in summer uniform. Just to reach us they had already lost four Alpini. On our journey, my diarrhoea did not give me peace and I had to stop every ten minutes. This debilitated me a lot, even though we were going downhill.

At a ruined farmhouse I met a captain and a major, one of them a medical officer. "Be careful, you have amoebic dysentery," he warned me. "But, luckily for you. your condition needs urgent treatment with immediate repatriation to Italy." I paid little attention to him and, finding a few grains of corn in my pockets, I lit a fire under a stone and made popcorn. After eating it with the two officers, we went on our separate ways.

I only stayed a few hours in Mali Trepelit. I was given some Atabrina anti-diarrhoeal pills, and took a plentiful supply with me. By now it was less cold, the rain had nearly stopped and it was easier to walk along the levelling path. At regimental command I found my transfer orders to the Julia and asked for my wooden case. The only clothes I possessed were the ones I was wearing. I was told a motorcycle was leaving immediately and jumped on it, but not before drinking a hot, delicious, coffee. The road was bad and we had to stop repeatedly because of my condition.

We made it to Valona, where I was finally able to take off those blessed gaiters, my mountain boots that had taken so much punishment and my socks. It was late and I went straight to bed. Finally a proper bunk bed. I later went to the mess, where all I wanted was soup and more soup. On leaving the hall, I realised that my Alpino hat, left on the coat hanger at the entrance, was missing its feather. It was a real eagle's feather, given to me by my Lucia before leaving for the front and I had become strongly attached to it. Livid, I took a beautiful feather from a captain's hat. Damn them! They wanted to screw me, now I would screw them. My hat with its new feather accompanied me through the Albanian campaign, then into Greece, before being finally lost in the sinking of the *Galilea*, in March 1942.

At Valona, I increased my supply of anti-diarrhoeal pills at a local field hospital. I then got a ride in a truck going to Mavrova, where I was transferred to the Julia division and then posted to the Gemona battalion of the 8th Alpini. I kept well away from doctors, and their "pernicious amoeba". It was the 9th February 1941 and that day I became part of the Julia.

Since I had left the Trento battalion I had given much thought to my situation. Every attempt had been made to keep me away from the front and I was considered a lunatic for wanting to take part in the fighting. I risked being "lost in action", or, worse, coming back in agonising pain, without a limb or disabled for life, as was the fate of many I saw. I should have made the same choice as my cousin who, based at general HQ in Tirana, would receive high decoration for talking about a war he never experienced in the real sense. Or another cousin, who remained in Rome as head of the royal palace guard and who was awarded the highest decoration for ... contracting 'flu while in service! I obstinately continued to seek to fight, despite all my contacts. My low opinion of these war-dodgers remained unchanged.

The Gemona was commanded by Maj Perrot. It had been decimated and temporarily pulled back from active duty to be reconstituted. On my arrival, I again met my friend Platone, with whom I had arrived in Albania. He had been posted to the Arditi platoon[7], which I had been really keen to join.

As I was the last officer to arrive in the battalion, I was given the responsibility of the mortar platoon: six 81mm mortars and 40 men. We learned almost immediately that we were due to be deployed on the southern part of the front, between Tepeleni and Cliusura, on the Vojussa river. In that area the fighting was at its most intense. If the enemy succeeded in breaching that sector, he would reach the Adriatic, isolate the Julia from the rest of the Italian army, and cut off supplies. What most concerned me, however, was getting rid of the amoebic diarrhoea without medical interference. My condition was beginning to seriously affect me and I knew that, besides bringing discomfort, it could prove fatal. I kept great trust in my pills though and, in the meantime, started learning more about mortars.

The Alpini who formed my mortar platoon were the so-called fortunate ones, who had been fighting since October 1940 and who were still around. It was there that I met Cpl Luciano Papinutti, who was to remain with me for the rest of that campaign and who joined me again on the Russian front. Under the guidance of Papinutti and other members of the platoon I learned about the use of the mortar, of which I knew relatively little. It is a fairly simple weapon, essentially a tube mounted on a steel plate, or base. It is relatively inconspicuous, easy to take apart and to transport, despite its weight. It is also simple to use: once the base is solidly resting on any flat surface, the tube is mounted, pointed and the range determined. The bomb is then dropped down the tube and its charge detonates when hitting the bottom, firing the shell towards the target in a steep parabola. Normal cover, such as thick walls or a mountainside, are ineffective against such a weapon, as it hits you from above without warning. Mortars proved to be deadly weapons, and were much used in Albania, Greece and Russia.

I met some fellow officers, one of whom was Lieut Ratto, who had already acquired a fearsome reputation in combat. He had single-handedly saved the 8th Regiment, then the entire Julia division, from encirclement.

"Where do you come from, Ferrante?" they asked.

"From the 11th Alpini, Trento battalion," I replied.

"Ah, so you know what war is." I was no longer a greenhorn for them.

I had been on the front line for 19 days, 456 hours of hard combat, but still considered myself a beginner when compared to those who had been here for 3 months. I became firm friends with Platone. As we both smoked pipes, one night we promised that, should one of us die, he would bequeath his pipe to the other. I also started to learn interesting little things. For instance, I learned how to delicately open a hand grenade, removing the safety catch and then the explosive, to make a container for tobacco or cigarettes. I was also informed that large carob beans, our fodder for the mules, reduced diarrhoea symptoms. "They narrow the intestine and you don't go for a whole week", I was assured.

I also finally managed to gain access to my wooden case and recovered a pair of long woollen underpants and a heavy sweater. The rucksack inherited from the dead Alpino was beginning to fill and I now had practically all I needed. I had lost some small objects that I considered of value, but many others, such as sunglasses, camera film and chocolate, I could now do without. What did concern me was that my Alpini still wore the summer uniforms in which they had started the campaign and that the Julia division, on the eve of being sent into combat again, had not received any winter supplies. I wrote to Rome about this predicament and in January received confirmation that Duchess Badoglio[8] had forwarded three large sacks of winter clothing in my name to our HQ in Tirana. They did not reach us until four months later, in May, when the weather had turned hot.

We also received many letters of support from young women in Italy, many with their photographs and addressed to "an officer of the Julia". Very nice they were too, but unfortunately many other "heroes" had opened them before they reached us on the front line and when they arrived they were all missing their photographs.

On the night of 22nd-23rd February we left Mavrova heading south-east, towards Tepeleni. Due to my condition, I was allowed to travel on a truck but, in order to relieve myself, had to count on the patience of the driver to make many stops. The weather could not have been worse, with cold temperatures and heavy rain. We passed Dorza and Sinanai and I had to continue on foot, crossing the Vojussa on a pontoon bridge. We left the road and the battalion continued on the bank of the river, on a steep and narrow path. We spent the night in a small Muslim village, where the houses had tiny windows with wooden grilles to allow women to look from the inside out but without being seen. The rain continued.

My mountain boots did not let me down and remained dry. Whenever I could, I rubbed anti-exposure fat on them. The following morning we continued our march, still in the rain, past Tepeleni and on towards the area where our units were to be engaged in combat. We found no shelter and spent the night hunkering between rocks, covering ourselves with ground sheets. The next morning I woke up drenched, but to my great surprise and greater joy realised my diarrhoea had gone!

I continued, nevertheless, to take those blessed pills up to May, five months in all. As a result, for the rest of the war and up to 1946, I remained immune from diarrhoea, which decimated so many of us on the Russian front. In addition, from that time I also avoided the unpleasant attention of bedbugs and lice, unlike my fellow soldiers who remained afflicted. I deduced that the pills had given a taste to my blood that those parasites could not stomach. Unfortunately, the lice were to return when I was wounded and a POW on the Don, in Russia in 1943, infecting me with typhoid.

OUR GOLGOTHA

CONTINUING OUR MARCH from Tepeleni, the valley narrowed into the gorge of the Vojussa river, bordered on the northern side by the Trebescine and Scindeli mountains and on the south by Mount Golico, which at that point fell vertically into the Vojussa. Golico's western side, towards Tepeleni, bordered on the river Drino, from which the slope at first rose gently, then became much steeper with shrubs and woodland, before ending in large slabs of rock. The summit was 1615 metres above sea level.

Mount Golico became known as Golgotha to us, because of the fighting that took place there between March and April 1941. We suffered heavy losses, as did the Greeks. The best unit of the Greek army, the Crete division, had been sent to our sector to reinforce numerous other units. They were confident they would annihilate the Italians. For some time Golico had been a theatre of hard fighting between their troops and our Sforzesca, Legnano and Ferrara infantry divisions and units of the Black Shirts (the Fascist militia). Our units had been worn down and decimated; it was now the turn of the Julia division to go into the breach.

We became familiar only with Golico's northern and western slopes. The enemy was solidly entrenched in positions at elevations of 1143, 1250 and 1531 metres above sea level on the eastern slope[9], and also occupied the summit, Position 1615. In addition, the Greeks had positioned heavy artillery in caverns a few kilometres to the south-west of Tepeleni, from where they were able to hit us with great precision. I informed our command of the shelling, but we were unable to counteract the fire as the exact location of the caverns was still unknown. We later started to receive heavy artillery hits from another direction and the first person to identify the source of the shelling was Papinutti, locating it by chance with his binoculars. We were being fired upon from our own sector, with our long-range 149mm guns! I immediately sent Papinutti to alert our artillery observation officer, who at first refused to believe him. As Papinutti later told me, the AO officer mocked him and blustered: "Only a few Greek shells! Is your section made up of cowards?"

Papinutti pointed to a precise point in our sector and insisted: "Look, Sir, they are firing at us from within our sector. Do you see that flash? Count to nine and the shell will arrive near us. Right there." The officer had seen the flash and started counting. As he reached seven an angry whistle grew, becoming quickly louder. For some reason, the gunners had adjusted their sights and the shell was about to hit us. Without a word Papinutti fell flat to the ground, and the AO officer dived into his observation post. The explosion was thunderous, after which the officer emerged, shaking and brushing earth from his uniform. "Fucking idiots," he said. "With your permission, Sir", Papinutti asked, "may I rejoin the cowards of my section?" But, rushing to telephone command, the officer was no longer taking any notice of him.

Figure 9: The summit of Mount Golico in March 1941
(photograph taken by an unknown Alpino)

We had been allotted five days' supplies of basic food, tack and tinned meat and some coffee. And, since leaving Mavrova two days before, neither officers nor men had received hot food or warm clothing, despite the foul weather. We were there to fight and die, because of the criminal incompetence of those who were convinced this would be a "stroll in the park". Gen Von Rintelen, when later describing to Hitler the Italian failures in north Africa, said: "We must add to the defects of the Italian operations the interference in military decisions of individuals who are incompetent in such matters, as has scandalously occurred at the beginning of the operations against Greece."[10] For all of us on the front line, the real enemies of the Italian army were our own general staff and politicians such as Badoglio, Jacomoni, Visconti

Prasca and especially the Foreign Minister, Galeazzo Ciano. In order to remain in Mussolini's favour, he did not hesitate to send soldiers to their doom.

While on Mount Golico, I was joined by Alpino Zamolo, who was allocated to me as my orderly. Zamolo turned out to be useless; he was only good at preparing coffee. He never lost an opportunity to vanish when the unit engaged in combat, when I most needed him. He was both cunning and work-shy and had thought that to volunteer to be my orderly was a master stroke. He had fulfilled this role for a military chaplain and was convinced that serving the officer commanding the mortar platoon would remove him from the dangers of the front line. Poor Zamolo! He remained with me during the whole terrible period when the Julia fought on Mount Golico and then he followed me into Greece.

On the 24th February, our Gemona, Tolmezzo and Cividale battalions, about 3,800 men in all, took up position on the steep northern slopes of Golico, with the Vojussa river behind them. The Vicenza and Aquila battalions were on the slopes of the Scindeli and Trebescine mountains, on the other side of the river.

On the morning of the 25th the Gemona started to make its way up Mount Golico, leaving the mules and the ammunition along the Vojussa gorge, out of reach of enemy fire. The Cividale had preceded us but had already sustained heavy casualties. As for the Tolmezzo, it was supposed to capture the summit (Position 1615), but it was still held up at 1531, which it had been unable to overrun. It was also caught up in a snow storm. We of the Gemona were lower down, clinging on to a gully that ran vertically down most of the mountain, the Death Gorge. We remained exposed to enemy fire from their Positions 1143 and 1250. The area had already seen heavy fighting, with positions being regained and lost several times. The Greeks knew of our arrival and had reinforced their lines, welcoming our arrival with heavy artillery and mortar fire and inflicting our first casualties. The rain had stopped, but the summit was covered with snow, peppered with black patches caused by artillery shelling.

I was trying to find the best location for my six mortars, not an easy task because of the steep slope. I eventually found emplacements for the heavy steel plates on which the mortars rested, aiming two of my weapons against Position 1143 and the other four against Position 1250, where we suspected the enemy had concentrated many troops. Then, with about 30 Alpini, I climbed down to the river to retrieve our ammunition, with each one of us climbing back up carrying six shells, weighing 3.5kg each. That was over 180 shells each trip.

On the path near the mules I met Lieut R, a career officer, who had slipped. He was making his way to the field hospital after grazing his knee. He was able to walk, but preferred to abandon the battlefield, as some others had done. Yet all of us there were risking our skins, having realised that life didn't count. I met him later during the war in Russia, where he was showing off a decoration obtained in the Greek campaign. It was probably given to him for escaping the carnage on Golico.

By the beginning of March the Cividale battalion had been almost completely annihilated. Of the thousand men fighting two days before, only around a hundred were left, despite the support of the Susa battalion. The Greeks, from their vantage point at 1531 metres, had managed to repel the Tolmezzo battalion as well. Its decimated troops fell back with enemy gun and mortar fire raining down. Death Gorge was under constant fire and full of bodies. I was in charge of our mortar platoon and, while my bombs were as deadly as theirs, the enemy had far more machine-guns and artillery and they continuously bombarded us from all sides and from above.

Through my binoculars, from behind boulder cover, I got occasional glimpses of the action on the other side of the Vojussa. About 500 metres to the north, units of the 9th Alpino regiment were clambering up Mali Scindeli mountain with great difficulty while the Greeks attacked from above. I sighted contingents of Black Shirts sent to support and reinforce the Aquila battalion, who, to my amazement, retreated almost as soon as they arrived. Full of rage and on my own initiative, I turned one of my mortars onto the Black Shirts' rearguard, where my bombs caused mayhem. I elected not to report this incident to anyone: but it left me with a profound sense of satisfaction, born out of contempt that had slowly matured against soldiers wearing berets. I had no idea whether I hit anyone or not, but I couldn't care less. They were fresh, newly arrived troops and they were already retreating.

Our units managed to resist the Greek attacks, despite severe losses. Between the 3rd and 6th of March, the Duce visited the front but kept his distance from our lines. Lieut-Gen Geloso ordered that: "current positions had to be defended man by man, metre by metre". He also expressed his profound trust in the abilities of the

"Julia division, which the whole Italian nation had learnt to admire". A few days later, War Bulletin No 275 informed Italy: "Armed Forces HQ informs us that there is nothing important to note from the Greek Front..."

However, for us these were terrible and agonising days. While out reconnoitring the area on the morning of 4th March, I found to my horror that, as I walked through Death Gorge, I kept tripping on bits of corpses in the snow. Once, I bent down to move what I thought was a stone, but it turned out to be a hand. From the snow emerged limbs and scraps of uniform, our grey-green mixed with Greek khaki, bodies blown apart by shrapnel and bullets. The luckier ones bled to death, the less lucky froze.

On my return I found my orderly Zamolo.

"What do you think about all this, Zamolo?" I asked.

"The same as you do, Sir."

"And what do you think that is?"

"The same as me, Sir!"

Gratified by this informative conversation, I sent Zamolo down the valley to load himself up with more munitions. Off he went, muttering all the way down. "Holy shit! Jesus fucking Christ!" And worse. His language might have been extreme, but it expressed only too well our state of mind in circumstances that were only too clear. Earlier in the campaign, with the Trento battalion, I had seen death, cold and hunger, but here all of these were concentrated on a single mountainside.

WE TAKE THE SUMMIT

WAR EXPERIENCED AT A DISTANCE, from Berati or Tirana, far from the front line, was very different. War was learnt on the front line, in the face of the enemy. There, men experienced what war really was. They never talked about it afterwards.

If I tried to say what it means to be a combatant, I would say that I possibly found the answer right here, in these mountains, where the complicated process of distilling this rare and special breed was achieved. Combatants live in a world unknown to others; a simple and illiterate world where the word hero, overused by the media and politicians, has no meaning. This is a world where war is represented by a tin of beef, if and when it reaches you, and by the diarrhoea that never leaves you, by the trousers that you never wash and the lice that become pointless to remove. War comes to be represented by shrapnel that buzzes angrily, by bullets that whistle overhead and by the lower sound they make when they just miss you, by an Alpino who cries: "*Mamma mia, Sior Tenente*", and then falls silent forever. It is represented by the blood of companions and enemies.

The beginning of March was one of the hardest periods. The enemy pressed relentlessly from above and from the east, aware of our exhaustion. They were determined to eliminate us. Positions were gained and lost. Casualties were severe on both sides. Capt Fregonara, of the Tolmezzo, fell while attacking the summit with hand-grenades, 2nd Lieut Brunengo, of the Cividale, despite being repeatedly wounded, returned to the assault and singlehandedly repelled the enemy. Both officers received the Medaglia d'Oro, the highest military decoration. Units of the Val Natisone and the Belluno battalions finally arrived to help us. The number of men and mortars under my command increased, but I found it difficult to keep track of who was under my orders. All around us too many died or vanished soon after arriving.

In Rome, our government could no longer ignore the seriousness of the situation and our high casualty rate. Mussolini did not miss the opportunity to focus the nation's admiration on the Alpini fighting in Albania, lavishing particular praise on the Julia. We were informed that dignitaries of the Fascist government were volunteering to join our front-line units. Sure enough, we were joined soon afterwards by the Minister of Public Works, Giulio Cianetti, and by the Minister of Education, Giuseppe Bottai.

They generally didn't last long. Cianetti, who joined us as an artillery captain, commanding the 13th battery of the Conegliano group, showed poor aptitude and became despised by his men. He even slapped our chaplain, Fra' Generoso, after incurring his criticism. But Bottai, who arrived as a colonel, commanding the Vicenza battalion, proved to be an excellent officer. I met him and came to share the admiration of his Alpini, as I also came to agree with their poor opinion of Cianetti. The latter was a megalomaniac who could not believe that we couldn't give a damn about Fascist high officials. After Bottai took command of the Vicenza, the battalion was no longer mentioned in reports, but it was the

"Minister who advanced", or "the Minister who had taken prisoners". With him, his Alpini had enough food and felt safer. He stayed with them, slept where they did, shared the same risks and took orders from his military superiors who, in Italy, would have stood to attention in front of him. He showed the true spirit of an Alpino officer.

On Golico, Positions 1143 and 1250 were still impregnable to us, despite all our efforts and the severe casualties on both sides. There was practically no cover on the steep terrain and it was nearly impossible to recover wounded, who died of exposure or blood loss. I continuously tried to move my weapons, as the Greeks were concentrating their fire on us, but it wasn't easy to move the mortars' 20kg steel bases and find other areas of ground flat enough on which to mount them again. The mortar barrels had become red hot and we were firing at less than 1000 metres.

We learned that the Greeks had broken through further east, reaching the road between Tepeleni and Cliusura. What remained of the Cividale battalion, together with units of Black Shirts and Bersaglieri had been unable to plug the gap, with the enemy artillery, machine-guns and mortars still clearly outgunning our forces. We turned our mortars and concentrated fire on the valley floor, joined by the artillery batteries of the Udine group and the Pusteria division. Luckily, at that time we did not lack ammunition.

Due to the piecemeal arrival of reinforcements, I now found myself in command of 18 mortars, instead of six, and 80 men. As the rough terrain did not allow us to make effective use of the additional mortars, on 5th March I was ordered to move part of my platoon to the opposite side of the valley. Leaving a detachment of my Alpini on Golico with Papinutti and Sgt Longaro to man the six original mortars, the rest of us left at night, carrying the other 12. At the bottom of the slope we crossed the Vojussa on the Dragoti bridge, which was being shelled by Greek artillery at three-minute intervals. We all made it to the other side and started to climb up Mount Scindeli. In exploring the area, we found a cavern large enough to shelter 50 men – it made me think of Ali Baba and the 40 thieves. I installed my Alpini in the cavern and put up my tent at its entrance, then positioned our 12 mortars not far away in a little ravine. From the entrance, I had a much better view of Golico and especially of positions held by the enemy. We started to fire, with mortar attendants being relayed every three hours. We aimed especially at Positions 1143 and 1250, now clear targets for my weapons. British planes dropped bombs, hoping at the same time to destroy the Dragoti iron bridge, but they missed. As usual, the Italian air force remained conspicuous by its absence.

I briefly crossed back over to Golico, to find out what was happening and especially to check how my Alpini were doing and how many casualties they had sustained. Cpl Papinutti had left with four men to place a mortar on Position 1250, which had just been retaken. I returned across the Vojussa and gave the new firing co-ordinates for the remaining mortars on Mount Scindeli. I was confident that we could annihilate the enemy, even if we lacked the high-explosive bombs which the Greeks possessed. The sun made a brief appearance, but the disputed positions were still covered with snow.

The enemy's pressure on Mount Golico increased, with attacks from all sides. The night of 6-7th March was unusually calm, with a dark sky and snow swirls that covered, without distinction, the living and the dead. At dawn, the Greeks launched an all-out attack near Position 1615, at the top of Death Gorge. Our boys were not taken by surprise and, when the fortunes of the fierce fighting seemed to turn against us, the Arditi platoon, commanded by my friend Augusto Platone, counter-attacked with hand-grenades and pushed back the enemy. But Platone, already wounded by mortar shrapnel, was mowed down by a machine-gun camouflaged between rocks.

That was the end of my friend, with whom I had set out from Bari and made the agreement that whoever died first would bequeathe his pipe to the other. We recovered his body and, after wrapping him in a blood-stained blanket, lowered him into a shallow grave in the small cemetery above the Dragoti bridge.

The fighting continued. Our orders were to resist at any cost and to use our bayonets if we ran out of ammunition, especially as supplies were dwindling. It was the morning of 7th March and 70th Company was ordered to halt the overwhelming Greek attack. It was led by the bold, invincible 1st Lieut Benvenuto Ratto, already decorated on the field three times. Everyone followed him into the assault, throwing hand-grenades and shouting "Savoia". Ratto fell, hit several times, but his men overran Position 1615, the summit of Mount Golico. That cursed position was finally ours. Ratto was posthumously awarded the Medaglia d'Oro.

One of my Alpini found Ratto's body in Death Gorge, among the many mutilated corpses. We buried him in the same small cemetery above the iron bridge, next to my friend Platone.

A LACK OF LEADERSHIP

OVER THE MONTH of March the Julia division continued to receive reinforcements to plug mounting losses, mainly survivors from decimated units. In my platoon, the number of men under my command was now above 100, but I was finding it increasingly difficult to keep track of them because of our regular losses and because they were deployed on both Mount Golico and Mali Scindeli, on either side of the Vojussa. The RAF and Greek heavy artillery continued to hit us unhindered.

Capt T arrived to take charge of my platoon, as we were more numerous than the whole battalion. I remember that during a Greek bombardment, in fear for his life, he stayed under an overhanging rock and called over to me: "Ferrante, one of your mortars has taken a direct hit and blown up the operators. You go and have a look. I lost these fingers to a bomb so I can't stand the sight of blood." I looked and found an Alpino with his head shattered and pieces of brain hanging on shrubs. Another, also dead, had a tiny wound near his heart. I recognised him as Alpino Cescatto, who only a few days before had asked me to help him write to his mother. He wanted to tell her that everything was going well and he would be back soon. Capt T, on the other hand, got a transfer back to command. In effect, setting another deplorable example as a career officer, he went back into hiding. He later arrived on the Russian front as a lieutenant-colonel.

I kept travelling over and back across the Vojussa, switching between being with my men on the Dragoti and those on Golico. Finally, I received permission to move one of my mortars on Golico to a strategic emplacement, close to Position 1250 and under a huge rock. It gave us access to the eastern slope which was still in Greek hands. On my way up I passed battalion command and saluted Lieut-Col Leonarduzzi, who said: "You are mad to place that mortar on that position!"

"It's all or nothing," I replied.

It was an ideal place. Even though the Greeks could still hit us, we could operate it at night, or when clouds protected it. I gave the firing co-ordinates and left seven Alpini, two to operate the mortar and the other five to lift shells.

Our chaplain, Fra' Generoso, wanted to see me and I wanted a word with him too. I wanted Platone's pipe, due to me according to our agreement. But the padre couldn't reach me, as, at the time, I had made a habit of going over the front line to relieve myself. There, with my backside exposed to our front line and facing the enemy, I had never had any problems. Fra' Generoso didn't dare come up to see me. However, Minister Bottai, commanding the Vicenza battalion, saw me with his binoculars. "*Tenente*, I have much admired your magnificent backside in observing our sector," he said. "Unfortunately, I did not have a rifle. Otherwise, I would have helped you in your dumping operations."

Figure 10: Transporting our dead Alpini in Albania

In the last days of March, conditions gradually started to improve. In our cavern on Mali Scindeli we regularly received food, post and ammunition, which was usually transported by mule. Since the beginning of military life, I had always had a particular affection for mules, and this increased with the experience of war. They arrived loaded with all the essentials and left carrying the wounded and the dead, on the most difficult terrain. And their steaks, cooked on an open fire, were delicious. I also had sympathy for the mule attendants, with their incessant cursing against God, Mussolini and high command on account of the lack of appreciation for their immense effort. And, perhaps aware of my feelings, they sometimes brought us supplies taken from our stores at Tepeleni after they were bombed: rice, pasta, tins of minestrone, quince jelly and parmesan cheese that, taken in a loaf of bread, had a taste that I never forgot. We finally had enough food. We had coffee and sugar and my Alpini were happy, except of course for Zamolo, who was still afraid to die with me, the poor devil.

The fighting continued for the whole of March, with the same high casualty rate. One day we noticed that the sun had started to appear more often and the cold was lifting. The smell from the corpses increased but, while the smell from animal remains could be endured, this was much more difficult to stomach, except by the crows, who feasted happily. The area near Death Gorge was especially foul.

Positions on Golico were taken, lost and retaken by both sides. As the fighting further south failed to produce any clear advantage, the Greeks resolved time and again to break through in our sector. The 18th and 24th of March were terrible, although they were finally crowned for us when the Gemona and Cividale battalions overcame the well-fortified Position 1143 by. On 31st March the enemy tried to retake Position 1615, but was repulsed with many losses.

THE ALBANIAN WAR ENDS

THE GREEKS HAD not given up and fighting continued into the beginning of April. The enemy registered a success in overcoming Position 1143 once more, but we also learned they were directing all their reinforcements eastwards, towards Salonika. The Germans, on 6th April, had crossed the borders of Yugoslavia, Bulgaria and Greece. German panzers, in pure *blitzkrieg* mode, cut through Yugoslavia and on 10th April occupied Zagreb. The day before they had already occupied Salonika, with the Greek Army of Thrace surrendering to them. On 20th April, the Commander of the 3rd Greek Army, Gen Tsolakoglu, agreed an armistice with the Germans.

Mussolini was mortified, even though Hitler announced that German success was in great part due to the Italian effort in tying down the main Greek units and facilitating the crumbling of the Greek army. A compromise was reached, with Gen Tsolakoglu surrendering to the Italian commander, Gen Cavallero, on 23rd April. Italy accepted the conditions dictated by Germany, including permission for Greek officers to keep their side-arms. The reply from Gen Von Rintelen to Italian protests was withering: "The Greek resistance and patriotism in fighting against Italy has impressed the world and it is only fair that the valour of this little nation be recognised."

This statement drew a line under a painful and humiliating chapter in the political machinations of Mussolini, the Foreign Minister and the Italian chiefs of staff. The war, sought by Italy, had been undertaken with poor intelligence, resources and organisation. Our army emerged weary and bloodied. It may have remained morally unscathed, especially the Alpini of the Julia, but at a terrible cost in terms of dead, wounded and missing in action. What had started as a "stroll in the park" became for Italy the bloodiest and most tragic page of the Second World War.

Just before Easter, on 15th April, the 8th Regiment received the order to leave Mount Golico and head for Saliari, where the Julia division had gathered, having been given three days to clean up. The fighting was over. On 20th April 1941, the bloody war between Greece and Italy officially came to an end. We left behind the land of the Vojussa, the Bescisti and the terrible Mount Golico, leaving so many of our people buried there. The few of us who had survived between February and April were dazed, incredulous and, at the same time, elated to be still alive.[11]

Snow and slush still lingered, but winter was on the wane. February, in Mavrova, was the last time we had seen all the units together and now we could admire the same filth, exhaustion and long beards in our colleagues that made us all look like brigands. But how many new faces were there, and how few of the original officers and men had survived. We learned that we had two new commanders, who had arrived just as hostilities had been suspended. We then received an inspection by Gen Carlo Rossi, a former Alpino and combatant in the Cividale battalion, who brought us the greetings of Mussolini and the admiration of the nation. He ended his speech with: "... and now that you are entering Greece, you have a free hand to get your own back and enjoy a well-deserved rest."

That is when a new set of troubles began for me though. The following morning, as I was busy trying to clean my shirt, I was summoned by Col Camosso, the new battalion commandant. He had no idea of what Golico had been for us. The colonel put me under house arrest for three days for failing to communicate the death of one of my Alpini. Under normal circumstances, this punishment would have been legitimate, but I felt I had plenty of extenuating circumstances: the Alpino had arrived at night, without notice, during a period of intense fighting and at a moment when it was impossible to keep track of who was arriving and who was missing. In addition, command posts only transmitted the names of newly arrived men when active combat ceased. I never knew – and still to this day do not know – the name of that Alpino. Command was uptight about my failure to communicate one death, when my problems at the time entailed finding replacements for 15 or 20 men who had gone missing!

I appealed and did not even get a hearing, but took this in my stride. After all that we had gone through – the suffering, the acceptance of death as inevitable, the fear of losing a limb or going permanently blind – being put under house arrest for a couple of days was not worth worrying about.

INTO GREECE

GEN CAVALLERO PASSED ON Mussolini's orders to us: "The Julia must enter Greece and proceed by forced march as fast as possible". The Germans' motorised columns had already reached central Greece, bypassing areas held by their Italian ally. But Hitler had his panzers and Mussolini had to make do with us Alpini, as reflected in one of our Alpini songs:

Motorizzati a pie',	(moving only on foot)
La plume sul ciapel,	(a feather in his hat)

> *Lo zaino affardellato,*   (a heavy rucksack on his back)
> *L'Alpino e' sempre quel*   (such is the Alpino forever)

Always the same story but, in this instance, poor Italy seemed even poorer.

We walked non-stop from Saliari half the length of the mountain chain in 48 hours, night included, at a rhythm of 50 minutes marching with 10-minute pauses every hour. It was no longer cold. The smell of carrion was overpowered by the sickly and nauseating stench of so many unburied bodies. We were aware of them from as far as 500m away, before we could even see them. In daylight, flocks of crows feeding on corpses also gave us warning. From then on and even more so in Russia, the sight of black crows rising from the dead caused me to despise those birds. Even when I was starving I couldn't eat them.

On the way we found a lot of materiel abandoned in retreat by the Greeks, especially ammunition. Their depots extended for hundreds of metres with great numbers of boxes. The biggest boxes were made in Britain, while the French ones often contained one very large shell each. I took one of these, disposed of its heavy contents and used it for my personal effects. Lower down on our left, towards the Drino valley, we found two heavy-calibre cannons well hidden in caves, almost certainly those that were shelling us on Mount Golico. Neither our air force nor our own artillery had managed to silence them. On the third day we were permitted to stop and to camp overnight. We were also given a hot meal. At the sight of all this abandoned materiel, one of my Alpini commented: "Look here, *Sior Tenente*, the only items missing are armchairs. It is lovely to go to war over here!"

We saw some small horses that had been tied together two by two by their front legs. No one was guarding them and, on remembering the words of Gen Rossi encouraging us to get our own back, I freed seven of them. To relieve my tired Alpini, I loaded them with weapons and ammunition. Suddenly Col Camosso appeared on his horse, elegantly dressed in black gloves, jacket and tie. He was clearly annoyed. He glared down on us, all sweaty and shirt-sleeved, and asked who had stolen the horses. "It was me, according to the instructions given by Mussolini through Gen Rossi, as it relieves my men", I replied. Camosso became even more irritated. My house arrest was extended. He was angry too to see us officers marching in shirtsleeves and without a tie. He, on the other hand, had travelled from Tepeleni by car and had then joined us – on a non-stop forced march – on horseback!

By 26th April we had travelled 150 kilometres, heavily loaded and across difficult terrain. That morning we arrived at Lake Gianina, well inside Greek territory, where our march finally ended. The Germans had already been here and had moved on a week previously. Our division was due to remain for four months, until the end of August.

So why had there been all this hurry to reach Gianina? We found out later that the Germans were moving quickly across Greece and the Italian authorities felt they had to show that we were not delaying either. Gianina was chosen because it was on the slopes of the Pindus mountains, in an area which the Julia had been about to reach at the end of October 1940, before pulling back because of a lack of men, ammunition and supplies.

We camped on the north-eastern side of the lake, in a field of magnificent beech trees. My orderly Zamolo was happy at long last: he realized he was not going to die with me. He readily busied himself boiling shirts, underpants and trousers, to eliminate the lice for both of us.

At the start of May I received in the mail two large bags (the third never reached us) sent by Duchess Badoglio from Rome in March. They had cagoules, heavy socks and scarves, all made by generous Roman ladies in wool, for "the poor Alpini suffering the cold". But they had arrived way too late and were useless in the warm weather. How much suffering and frostbite they would have saved had they arrived within a couple of weeks? I wrote back politely thanking the Duchess – and passed on the clothing to local shepherds.

We were camped on the northern side of Lake Gianina, which was maybe 1km wide. One night we found a small boat and rowed across to the other side to hunt for frogs. My Alpini repeatedly warned: "But they will shoot against us, *Sior Tenente*, if we don't know the password!" Nothing transpired. On our return, we quickly fried some frogs' legs in butter from our 5kg boxes. I have rarely eaten anything more delicious.

All those who had fought on the Albanian front were awarded a commemorative medal, a cross featuring the Skandenberg coat of arms of the 9th Army. We passed our time exercising. Each unit formed its own football team. I especially remember the newly arrived and very active Lieut Galigaro. Nicknamed the Lion of

Pindus, he was boastful and good-natured. He had never fought on Mount Golico.

SACRED RELICS

DURING MILITARY EXERCISES with my platoon, we reached the slopes of the Pindus range. By chance we came upon an old monastery, dilapidated and badly damaged by the German troops, among others, who had preceded us. On the floor amid the rubble I found a small icon. It was covered with metal except for the face of the Christ, which was painted. His crown was missing. It had possibly been made of precious stones that had been wrenched off. Further down the aisle, I noticed that the small, double wooden doors that separated the faithful from the sanctuary was very old, and had beautiful panels painted in miniature. Realising the church's state of abandon, I resolved to move the door somewhere safer as it belonged more in a museum than in this chaos. Also, half buried in the rubble, we found an old wooden case with vestments, a silver chalice and an old missal with silver corners on the cover and pages of finely decorated parchment. All were wrapped in a drape of red damask. We decided to return so a couple of days later we came back, unhinged the door, loaded it on to a mule and put the missal and chalice in a rucksack with the damask.

Back at the camp an Alpino carpenter made a sturdy case for the doors, to await our return to Italy. However, when returning from exercises the following day, we discovered that the case with the doors had vanished. Shortly after, I was summoned to the presence of the commandant of the division, Gen Girotti. Surprised, I went to his large tent, where I was shown in to the general, who reproached me bitterly: "How can an officer such as yourself, with a degree in law, steal the property of others? The archimandrite of the monasteries of the region has lodged a complaint. What do you have to say in your defence?" Without awaiting my reply, he snapped: "Go and await orders." I went away with my tail between my legs, but I would have liked to comment that those doors were exceptional, dating back to the 7th or 8th century and that many others would have been tempted to remove them. Also, I still had the chalice, the icon and the missal.

Should I hide them, or go back to the general and tell him? What if they were found?

The missal and the chalice were lost in the sinking of the *Galilea*, together with all my belongings. The little icon survived with me and made its way to Italy, where an antiquarian confirmed it was old and rare. The dark metal covering it proved to be silver.

Going back to where my tent had been, I realised it had been removed and set up in isolation. The order was that I should remain alone and under arrest: my meals were brought to me and nobody could talk to me. Nevertheless, I still participated in exercises and manoeuvres with my unit.

My Alpini brought me a fox cub they had just captured. I named it Pindo, baptising it with a lot of water, because it smelled. Pindo's stay was short-lived. During the night the cub was very noisy and during the day, when Zamolo put it on a lead to take it for a stroll, it always tried to escape and it still smelled powerfully. I decided to set it free.

In the meantime, a strange thing happened. All the units of our division received the order to form groups of their best officers and men, for an eventual parade in Athens. The Gemona battalion chose me. How could this be? I had been punished and isolated and everybody knew the crimes I had committed. Now everything was changing, even though they kept me a few more days in isolation. So, was I a good officer? I was once again in the same predicament I was after my raid on the French fort. Was I to be demoted or commended? My colleagues and I were bewildered. My battalion commander, Lieut-Col Martini, pretended nothing had happened and continued to treat me well.

Tactical exercises continued and one day we were asked to explain to the officers of the 8th Regiment how the 81mm mortars worked. Together with other chosen units we took part in a demonstration, and my Alpini were proud to be chosen as the best. Capt T, the same officer who had earlier asked me to take charge as he couldn't stand the sight of blood, started to explain the mortar's pointing mechanism to all the officers, but got into a muddle. Papinutti said to him, quietly: "Excuse me Sir, that last bit was back to front." The captain turned on him: "What would an ignoramus like you know? Shut up!"

Papinutti looked at me and I winked at him, meaning to keep quiet and not to worry. As soon as the captain had finished, I politely asked the officers present to let my Cpl Papinutti carry out a demonstration. We aimed the mortar at a target 3,800 metres away and started firing, hitting it on our second shot, to everyone's admiration. Later that same evening, a group of officers went to Papinutti's tent. "Sorry, Corporal, but would you mind explaining to us what the captain said earlier?" one asked. From then on Papinutti, who was already known as an expert, became known as *Il Mago del Mortaio* (the mortar magician).

After this lucky episode I was fully readmitted to my unit and it was as if nothing had happened. In the evening at the officers' mess, plenty of bets were made on me. Fra' Generoso was laying a wager that I would find out where the doors of the monastery were kept and retrieve them; Veterinary Lieut Campese was saying that Ferrante would once again cross the lake in his little rowing boat, but instead of hunting frogs he would raid divisional command to recover the holy doors.

We laughed and drank at these jokes, but I still wondered who had taken the doors and was probably laughing at me now. I was sure there was more to the complaints of the archimandrite than met the eye. When going on exercises with my platoon, battalion command felt it necessary to add two carabinieri (military police) to my unit. Lieut Ferrante, I thought, must be really terrible, but my Alpini were proud to be with me. They were always cursing, but I remained with them and was in turn proud of them and of what we had gone through together. The old hands, those who had gone through the whole Albanian campaign, each deserved a monument back in Italy. Now that no more enemies were around, they emerged as simple, frank and open people.

In the meantime, I had received my new dagger from Rome, after the previous one went missing heaven knows where. I had the motto of one of my Alpini engraved on the blade, "*Anin, varin fortune*" ("let's go, we will be lucky")[12]. I couldn't know at the time that the motto would be realised during my return to Italy on the *Galilea* and during the Russian campaign.

"Tell me, what is a hero?" I asked.

"Well, *Sior Tenente*, the hero can only be in Rome, if he is alive. If he is dead, he went missing on Mount Golico. The difference is this: in Rome he will never have seen the war and if he's on Golico, he's lucky he will never go to Rome. For fuck's sake! True, *Sior Tenente?*"

We ran circles around the two carabinieri who were attached to us. One day we found ourselves in a meadow full of sheep.

Imagine the Alpini among the lambs! But the shepherd was one of those to whom we had given the two bags full of winter clothing sent by Duchess Badoglio and we reached a mutually satisfactory agreement with him. As a result, Alpino Gatti was chosen to elegantly slaughter a lamb with my brand new dagger. It was roasted on the spot over a good fire. A portion was also given to the two carabinieri who, upon our return to base, obviously had nothing to report.

In July we left at dawn for Metzovo, the area where the Julia division had arrived in October 1940 before having to retreat. Rome had given authorisation for a show to be organised to celebrate this event, and the divisional and battalion commands attended, arriving by car. Fra' Generoso and Veterinary Lieut Campese were ordered to remain with the mules, while the rest of us were ordered to go on foot. I did not appreciate the 40km round trip to get there. Worse, I did not like the show: the girls were ugly and I would have gladly put that draft-dodger of a presenter against the wall to be shot.

We started to hear through the grapevine that we would soon be on the move again, maybe to Athens. We were waiting only for the trucks to transport us.

LAST DAYS IN GREECE

IN AUGUST, WE FINALLY received the order to move south. We travelled by truck through Trikkala and Samia, past ancient monasteries crowning inaccessible rocks. The only way in was via nets winched from above with pulleys. We reached Athens and camped near there, but too late for the victory parade. Two days later we passed the port of Piraeus and reached the small village of Istmia, where the battalion had been ordered to garrison the eastern end of the Corinth canal. We planted our tents among pistachio trees, whose foliage shone a light green.

Life on the canal proved to be monotonous. Many of us had already gone home on leave – 15 days at home plus the travelling time. I was also waiting to go, but was worried about the missal, icon and chalice. I did not dare leave them to anyone.

The Greeks gave us no trouble, but they had little food. We Alpini helped out when we could. A woman cleaned the house where I was billeted with another officer and we gave her enough to feed her family. We did the same with another woman who did all our laundry. Zamolo was always with me, but I only saw him in the mornings, when he brought me coffee. Every day Lieut-Col Martini used to let me ride his horse, a superb thoroughbred. To remain active, we also fished – with hand-grenades. The results were unsatisfactory until we tried using mortar bombs. They were much better and everyone was enthusiastic, including the Greeks.

We had strict orders to guard the road to Piraeus and Athens and, of course, the canal itself and its two ferries. No one was allowed across without a pass. One morning, a large German car with a flag fluttering arrived near our ferry. The driver, speaking in German, ordered our corporal to ferry his general to the opposite side. The corporal answered, in Friulano dialect: "And your documents?" The general got out of the car and shouted, ordering his immediate passage, but got nowhere. Not even the Almighty was going to cross the canal without a pass, according to our man. Two Alpini on the ferry aimed their guns at the car. The general had to turn back. Two days later, a note of commendation for our stand arrived from the German command. It was addressed to the Italian unit at Istmia and was read out to all the men.

I managed to visit Athens with my colleague Francesconi and we went to the German embassy. Everyone there was courteous and I was able to give them a letter to forward to my family in Dresden. Later, we found two good-looking local girls and managed to spend a small fortune with them. Athens was a fascinating city, but its inhabitants were starving. As we left one of the best pharmacies, the owner ran after us. He asked us to try to get some bread for his family, as he could not make ends meet. Many wounded and disabled Greek soldiers were also walking the streets, having arrived from the areas where we had been fighting. The people knew who we were and at first looked at us with loathing but, over time, they came to realise that the Alpini were simple, mountain people, much the same as them. We did not hate the Greeks and had no real responsibility for starting this war, which they also detested.

Before going on my 15 days' leave, I learnt the Greek song "*Koroido Mussolini*" (coward Mussolini). We sang it under the tent at night. Our commander, Lieut-Col Martini, pretended not to hear.

Try as I might though, I couldn't feel admiration for the *Euzones*, the crack Greek mountain troops. They guarded the royal palace wearing skirts coloured ivory, with pleats. Then again, who knows, maybe they thought our feathered hats were equally ridiculous.

At last, I received my 15 days' leave. On departing Corinth for Bari on the *Galilea*, Lieut-Col Martini asked me to deliver a box of personal effects to his family in Italy. I arrived in Bari, forwarded the box and continued by train to Naples, to see my *nonni* (grandparents). I reached the city just as it was being bombed by the RAF. All services were suspended. Used to bombing and with that fatalism of the front line, I put on my rucksack, with a 10kg oil can for my girlfriend, and started out on foot. I crossed the city, passed the royal palace, went along the seafront and reached Posillipo where my *nonni* lived unscathed. I was only a couple of hours late. On the way, I was amused by people peering at me from basement windows, shouting: "He's totally crazy!"

After a – too brief – visit to my girlfriend in Carmagnola, near Turin, I travelled north across the border to Dresden to visit my parents. There, my father managed to have my leave extended. Afterwards, I returned to Italy via Carmagnola and Rome, until finally, on 10th January 1942, I reached Bari, to embark for Greece and rejoin my battalion. Bari was still the same squalid hole, with soldiers transiting the city en route for Greece or Yugoslavia. I found a room at the Albergo Oriente, but realised that the local command was sending most of the soldiers destined for Greece to the new polyclinic, which was still unfinished. It had no doors, the windows were without panes and the walls had no plaster. I protested with command and was told: "You're used to sleeping on the ground when on the front line. You can do it here too". I said: "With respect, these men with me have risked their lives for you people. And this is how you treat them? This is a disgrace!"

I stayed a month in Bari, waiting to learn my departure date. Other ships had arrived, but the men were still on board, and had to remain there, for up to several weeks. At the start of February many shipwrecked soldiers arrived. It was obvious that, apart from our efforts being disorganised, the sea "was very dirty" – military jargon for the serious risk of being sunk by enemy action. The weather had turned cold, and with that came rain and slush. The men in the polyclinic were suffering. Several of them fell ill and had to go to a real hospital. I spent all my money and the *nonni* from Naples had to bail me out, twice.

To pass the time, I went to the dentist and had two fillings replaced and my teeth cleaned. When I asked for the bill he replied: "You don't owe me anything. I see you're in the Julia division. It is we who are in your debt." I was moved, as nowhere in Italy had I received any acknowledgement of our fighting. In Germany, it was another story. When I was in a tram in Dresden even old people stood up insisting that I sit. In Italy, almost nobody cared an iota.

We finally sailed from Bari on 11th February and stopped off in Corfu to join a larger convoy. I rejoined the Gemona in Lutraki, another town on the Corinth canal. Shortly afterwards we were joined by new recruits, the fifth time this had happened since the start of the Albanian campaign.

Lutraki was a holiday resort with 47 hotels and many of the Alpini were billeted there. They kept us in training and we tried to imitate the German goose-step, while singing Alpino mountain songs. Few tunes could be adapted to the march, but the results were magnificent and my Alpini professed themselves enthusiastic. Every day, when we received our food, large numbers of children congregated around us and we gladly gave them what we could.

I had become friends with a Greek ship-owner who lived in a villa by the sea and got a fantastic exchange rate in Italian lira from him for my uncle's US dollars. The Greeks wanted dollars and were not interested in marks or lira.

Rumours were commonplace that the Julia would soon be repatriated to be deployed elsewhere. On 10th March, the 8th Regiment was reviewed by Gen Geloso, commander of the army in Greece, who confirmed our departure. We were slow to believe him but, over coffee with my Capt Bonello at the ship-owner's villa, our Greek friend stated categorically that we would leave before the end of the month. "But how do you know of this?" I asked. "That is what they say in Athens," he replied. But he would not comment further. I was surprised that he knew and, much later, in my report on the sinking of the *Galilea* I commented on the lack of discretion regarding such an important troop movement.

On 27th March at 7am the Gemona battalion started to embark on the *Galilea*. The full battalion boarded, 1,300 men in all, together with another 150 to 200 of the regimental command. A few men going on home leave, 64 political prisoners and six women, being sent to Italy with an escort of 12 carabinieri and their NCO, completed the passenger roster. Including crew, the ship's complement was between 1,600 and 1,700 souls.

Because of a lack of space, most of the men were billeted in the four holds, with the remaining Alpini occupying both the fore and rear decks. Feeling unlucky, they had to try to find shelter from the light rain. Each man was handed a life jacket, and was told to wear it, and was given the necessary instructions about keeping shoes untied, not smoking at night on open decks and discarding immediately anything that could impede movement in an emergency. I was given a cabin to share with Lieut Campese on Deck C. The temporary commander of the Gemona, 1st Capt D'Alessandro set up four-hour shifts, on which patrols of an officer with 12 men went about the ship to ensure good order.

The *Galilea* finally set sail and was joined by another five ships, escorted by four torpedo boats and a few planes to check our route. We were all happy to be on our way back, to our families and our homes. A ship's officer told me that almost all the crew had experienced incidents at sea. "It is well known," he said, "that, if anything happens, you must abandon ship immediately. Only those who do so have a chance of surviving." He went on to say that, as for him, he had no fear, being a long-distance swimmer. He had been a member of the Italian Olympic swimming team. He would not be among the survivors.

On leaving the Gulf of Patras, the ships advanced in chessboard formation, with the largest ship, the *Piemonte* ahead. Towards 18.30 hours, sitting at a table, we jumped as a depth charge launched by one of our escorts exploded too close to the surface. From then on, a sense of nervousness crept over us, as we realised we were in an area where enemy submarines lay in ambush. Officers and NCO's went to reassure their units, but I noticed that crew-members remained nervous. After visiting my mortar platoon, I went to the boat deck with Luciano Papinutti, climbed into a lifeboat and found a box of Nestle condensed milk tins. (I had noticed on a previous crossing that each lifeboat had two of these boxes.) Helped by the darkness, we brought the box back to our platoon, who divided the tins among themselves.

All was quiet. In the salon, a gramophone played classical music. As soon as I finished my shift and handed over to another officer, I went down the two flights of stairs to my cabin on C Deck. Lieut Campese was already lying in his bunk, fully dressed and in his life-jacket. He was fast asleep. I stripped, put my pyjamas on and went to sleep.

4: *GALILEA*

THE SINKING

A FEW EVENTS in our lives mark us deeply, events that later come back to haunt us with a frequency and intensity proportionate to what happened. The sinking of the *Galilea*, in which nearly all of my Gemona battalion vanished beneath the waves, is one such event.

Figure 11: S/S Galilea, 8040 tons, sunk in the Ionian Sea on 28 March 1942

28TH MARCH 1942, 22.40 HOURS

AWOKEN by a dull explosion, I saw Lieut Campese, with whom I was sharing my cabin, already up and ready to leave.

From that moment, we all had peculiarly individual experiences. We lived terrifying and what seemed like endless moments all of which felt entirely differently from one person to the next. All I can narrate is what happened to me, what I heard, saw and felt, physically and emotionally.

"What's up?" I asked Campese.

"Get out and get a move on", he said. "The ship's been hit."

I did, but that was the last I saw of Campese.

The ship was already listing significantly and I rushed along the corridor in my pyjamas, bare-footed and without a life jacket. I knew I had to make my way to the bow where a stairway led up to A Deck.

According to the official report on the sinking (issued only several decades later), the ship was hit starboard by a torpedo towards the bow, immediately beneath the bridge. The torpedo apparently penetrated the hull and exploded as it reached the other side, puncturing a large hole. Water gushed in, making the ship tilt to port, the side where our cabin was situated. The ship's engines, however, continued to run and she drove on through the night. At the moment of impact, the *Galilea* was about five to ten miles from the coast, near the islands of Paxos and Antipaxos, south of Corfu. Water depth in the area is between 1,000 and 2,000 metres.

The ship's electricity supply, like the engines, was still working so the watertight doors automatically closed. This meant that the Alpini in all four holds had no chance of escape. An iron door closed in front of them forever. I could feel their panic and terror. The words of a survivor cannot describe the devastating feeling, the overwhelming energy caused by total panic, that they must have felt.

Outside of the holds, finding ourselves alone and isolated, screaming, confusion, and fear broke out as we realized our impotency in the face of death – a sensation we Alpini were unaccustomed to. At the same time, a black, stormy sea combined with rain, wind and thick fog to increase our anxiety and sense of desperation.

The other vessels in the convoy, following well-established naval regulations, had fanned out in compass shape to avoid serving as a further target. Only a small destroyer, the *Antonio Mosto*, stayed close by but, due to the rough seas, was unable to come alongside. In brief moments of visibility we thought we could make her out.

AROUND 23.00 HOURS

SLOWLY, THE *GALILEA* sailed on. Then, all of a sudden, her engines stopped.

According to the official report, the ship's officers "made great efforts to restore calm, to silence the troops and to show them how to save themselves…" This does not correspond to what I experienced. I never saw or heard the officers. Neither did I see any evidence that the captain "attempted to bring the ship towards land and possibly run her aground going against the wind". Not one of the senior officers was saved and many lost their heads, including the naval officers. Not one of them tried to help the soldiers, women and civilian prisoners who were on board. The official report was total fiction.

Once I reached the covered walkway on the starboard side of A Deck, directly underneath the boat deck, I found a crowd that had congregated on this side of the ship (it was listing strongly to port). Through the mist I could make out Capt D'Alessandro on the bridge who, in full dress uniform, was shouting through a megaphone: "Everyone must abandon ship, immediately. Long live the King! Long live the Duce and long live Italy!" A second later I saw him throw himself into the sea, complete with hat, belt and mountain boots. He immediately disappeared below the waves.

The chaos eliminated all levels of authority and rank. All men were rendered equal and all were equally intent on saving themselves. The convergence of so many people on the boat deck to gain access to the life-boats turned into a disaster. The disorder caused by the panicked rushing for boats meant they were useless. I saw an overflowing boat crash into the sea and break up. Another one, just above my head and just as full, was held by its prow on a fixed rope when the rope holding the stern was released. The boat fell vertically into the water throwing out everyone aboard. Another boat remained tethered to the ship by a rope and it crashed repeatedly against the hull, crushing all those between the two.

Capt Bonello, leader of my command company, lost his head. Leaning over the parapet, he threw himself into the sea while still holding on to a rope hanging over the side. The engines were still partially running when he disappeared, probably cut to pieces by the propellers.

On the walkway, Lieut-Col B, of the 8th Alpini command was equally overcome. He drew out his pistol and shot himself in the head. He was one of those who, during the battles at the foot of Mount Golico, used to hide in his tent in fear. Majs Savorè and Ubaldi, both from Command Division, also disappeared. Savorè had his head crushed between a life-boat and the side of the ship.

I reached the covered walkway on A Deck whose windows looked out over the sea. In the dark, I saw a collapsed Alpino who was groaning and covered in blood. He had broken the thick glass in one of the windows and, leaning through it to throw himself into the sea, had slashed open his stomach. I couldn't save him.

I returned to the open deck massed with despairing men. The screams and agitation left me strangely unaffected. I found myself isolated, overtaken by an unusual sense of calm.

Increasingly convinced that the *Galilea* would capsize, I caught hold of a rope and lowered myself towards the sea without a life-jacket. A wave lapped at my feet and, looking around me, I saw bodies floating on the surface. The water was cold and menacing. I quickly changed my mind, climbed back up the sloping side of the ship and pulled myself over the rail.

AROUND 23.20 HOURS

THE *GALILEA'S* ENGINES had, by now, stopped for good. Little more than half an hour had passed since we had been hit but they had been terrible and seemingly interminable minutes.

Suddenly, I heard Luciano Papinutti behind me: "*Signor Tenente*, what can we do?"

I said it was our duty to save ourselves and abandon this confusion. "What's more", I added, "come with me. I've left my torch and knife in my cabin. We could use them to make a raft. I must get them."

"Wherever you're going, I'm coming too", he said.

My cabin was two decks below on the side of the ship that was leaning into the sea. I imagined that by now it would probably be already full of water. The two of us ran down the main stairway and along the internal corridors. The night-lights were still lit. We moved with great difficulty as the ship lurched about, but made it to the cabin. From above my bunk I took my knife, which I gave to Papinutti, but also my torch and my Leica. "The ship hasn't sunk yet", I thought, "and I may well need these."

On our return up the corridor, forced to hang on to the handrail due to the severe list, we discovered to our horror that the watertight door had closed in front of us. Luckily, though the door was heavy, the automatic lock had not worked as, by then, the electric circuits were dead. Working together, we managed to force it open just enough to squeeze through. We climbed the main stairway and found ourselves out in the open again, among nightmarish scenes of terror and thoughtless mayhem. The horror of sinking contrasted absurdly with the chaos.

Still with Papinutti by my side, I worked my way towards the stern where we knew some life-rafts were kept. We were joined by another solitary and disoriented Alpino, Angelo Forte. Once there, we realized we couldn't launch the rafts because of the strength of the sea and wind. Forte left us to look for another solution elsewhere. I went with Papinutti to the very stern and we sat out in the open under the rain and wind with a group of Alpini already there. From above, we could hear the cries of those trapped in the holds: a porthole had possibly been broken but it would still be too small for a man to get out. They were all condemned to die.

The Alpini I had joined appeared to have lost hope and even my friend Papinutti left us to look for another means of saving himself. Someone covered me with a blanket but I felt neither the cold nor the rain. Feeling doomed, all those sitting began to recite the Rosary. I forbade them to pray, still convinced we could be saved. We could not afford to lose hope. I considered going down to the dining room and bringing them back a bottle, but another lurch of the ship dissuaded me.

Both Papinutti and Forte rejoined me and the Alpini. Nearby, we sighted a small, upturned lifeboat. Looking more closely, I spotted some ropes. At the far end of the *Galilea's* prow I spotted a couple of sailors who could have helped us, but they were so drunk they were of no use. So, we organised ourselves, turned the boat upright and attached two lengths of rope, one at each end. Papinutti helped me with the knife. While lowering it into the choppy sea by hand, one of the ropes slipped and the boat fell vertically towards the water. We managed to pull it back up, knotted the rope better, and finally settled it on the sea's surface. Twelve Alpini let themselves down into the boat. We quickly found that one of the two oars was missing.

Here is Papinutti's recollection of these moments: "*Lieut Ferrante ordered me to lower myself down into the lifeboat and take charge, but I refused. "I'm staying with you," I replied. Ferrante repeated his order, adding that, as the last officer aboard, he had to stay until all the Alpini had evacuated the ship. "But I know nothing of boats and the sea," I replied, "and neither does anyone else, apart from you." Ferrante then climbed down into the boat and immediately called: "Papinutti, come down." But, as I was about to lower myself, two other Alpini pushed ahead and went aboard instead. The little boat looked overcrowded by now, so I called to Lieut Ferrante: "There is no more space, I'll stay here. Promise me that you will come back for me." "You have my word," he said, and started pushing the boat away from the sinking ship. It soon disappeared into the fog.*

The minutes passed, then half an hour. The water was about to reach the deck. Suddenly I heard a faint shout: "Papinutti!" I shouted back "Ferrante", as loudly as I could. I heard "Papinutti" another couple of times and again answered, but couldn't tell whether he could hear me. Then, silence.

The ship lurched further and the water reached the deck. I tied my life-jacket tighter and helped the other two Alpini left with me to do the same. Then I let myself go into the water. "It's not too cold," I told the other two, "come on!" and started to swim as best I could and as far away from the ship as possible, to avoid being sucked under when the Galilea sunk. The other two did not follow me and I never saw them again.

I found a plank of wood, which I grabbed and told myself I still had a decent chance of being found. Then, suddenly, the dark shape of the destroyer Antonio Mosto was in front of me. I shouted as loudly as I could. From the ship they lowered a net, which I tried to grab but failed because of exhaustion and the waves. On my third attempt I caught it, and let go the plank of wood. My head went under, but I held tight and was hauled on board.

One of the sailors gave me a heavy pullover and led me inside. There I confirmed that the Galilea had finally sunk. I asked if any officers had been saved. The crew was busy, but one of them said: "We may have found one. Have a look in the cabin below." I went down and found Ferrante flat on the captain's bunk. He regained consciousness and saw me: "Papinutti, what are you doing here?" I replied that, as he had been unable to join me I had decided to join him instead. He then noticed that my face was chalk white and said: "The toilet is over there." I reached it just in time and was very sick.

Continuing my own recollection of my last moments on the *Galilea*, I remember someone shouting to me to come down to guide the lifeboat. I did, but only after reassuring those remaining, among them Papinutti, that I would come back to save them. In fact, I had spotted the small destroyer sailing through the fog nearby. At the bow of our lifeboat was Forte. I gave him my torch since he was a telegraph operator and could point the SOS in the destroyer's direction.

Still in my pyjamas and with my Leica round my neck, I tried to get the lifeboat away from the *Galilea* with our one oar. The current, and possibly the wind, came to my aid. Although beginning to suffer from painful cramps, I struggled weakly on. We could clearly see through the fog that the destroyer was approaching, trying to come alongside us. We finally managed to get the Alpini from the rowing boat on to the destroyer and, since I had promised those left on the ship that I would go back for them, I shouted again and again for a sailor to bring another oar and accompany me back to the *Galilea*.

A volunteer finally appeared. With both of us rowing, we made our way towards the sinking ship. We thought we could occasionally see it through the darkness of the waves. However, it was difficult getting back with the sea filled with floating bodies. We loaded up 12 who were howling, and so still alive. My cramps were becoming more intense and I had no strength to shout out and encourage those left on the ship. We returned to the *Mosto* that had followed us and, for the second time, those saved were taken on board. Then I lost consciousness …

When I came to I was lying on the bunk of the destroyer's captain and Papinutti was standing beside me. He was in his underpants but was also wearing a woollen jerkin, given to him by a crew member. He still had my dagger and announced that the *Galilea* had sunk at around 03.50hr with all remaining personnel on board. Many people had elected to remain on the ship, in addition to the unfortunate men locked in the four holds. They did this out of fear or because they had gone out of their minds.

Unfortunately, the wind rose further, the waves climbed higher and the temperature dropped. Some survivors still in the water succumbed to hypothermia and drowned. The *Mosto* continued to navigate in the area and rescued a few more. At dawn, a periscope was spotted and our vessel tried to ram it. It turned out to be a listing sloop with Lieut Minini in white T-shirt and underpants, holding an oar upright to attract attention. The *Mosto* barely avoided a collision and saved him too.

Around 8.30 we were joined by two minesweepers and torpedo boat No 516, which had set sail from Prevesa, the closest Greek port. They continued to pick up survivors and bodies. Two seaplanes appeared, trying to locate survivors, but their contribution proved useless. One crashed into the sea and the other soon disappeared. So much for our air force.

The rescue operations continued until early afternoon and I managed to take an exposure with my wet Leica of the Alpini rescued by the *Mosto*, hoping the camera still worked. We were then taken to Prevesa where, as soon as we landed, another survivor died. We counted ourselves: of a total of 1700 on board, 203 had survived, of whom 143 were with the Gemona.

We went to the town square, where 43 bodies recovered from the sea were laid out, among them Lieut Campese, with whom I had shared the cabin and the campaign. It was eerie to see the corpses without any signs of suffering. I remember that Campese was smiling. He was buried in the local cemetery alongside the other drowned Alpini.

My orderly Zamolo had vanished, I presumed lost along with so many other Alpini on the *Galilea*. But his strong self-preservation instinct had not deserted him and he had embarked on another ship, before safely returning to Italy.[13]

CONCLUSIONS

FROM PERSONAL RECORDS and photographs taken with my Leica, which I had managed by chance to keep with me during the sinking, I was able to recount events with great clarity. However, my own narrative cannot constitute the sole and definitive reconstruction of the sinking, as each survivor has his own story, with very personal moments. I apologise for recounting only the events that I witnessed personally, which remain crystal clear in my mind, and for perhaps obfuscating terrible episodes experienced by others. All the survivors, without exception, came out of it through sheer luck, regardless of moral or physical valour. Few of those Alpini had any experience of the sea.

The general staff in Rome requested an official report of the sinking. This was written on the basis of the report by the only surviving career officer, Lieut Bernardinis. For operational reasons and to preserve morale, the initial report had not been able to provide an accurate and comprehensive description. The official report by the Italian navy was only issued in 1995, half a century after the end of the war and 53 years after the sinking of the *Galilea*. Being produced mainly by personnel who had not participated and given the long delay, this report has many errors and misunderstandings. I therefore feel that a person who witnessed the event should bring some necessary clarification.

1.   The authorities contend that the sinking could have been better managed, saving many more passengers. Today, they say, this could not happen. Nothing could be further from the truth. The sinking occurred at night, in fog and in very rough seas and today, very much as yesterday, human beings are helpless against extreme forces of nature. In this sense, a tragedy at sea is no different to an earthquake or avalanche. This situation was also unusual in its own right, given that the passengers were mostly mountain troops, few of whom could swim. However, it should be noted that the intervention by the Italian air force did come too late and it proved to be ineffective.

2.   The report implies that the Navy could have done better. However, the few survivors said that naval personnel on board were experienced and had been exposed to similar situations, only in these extreme circumstances they were unable to assist at all. The young naval officer to whom I had spoken that night had been part of the Italian Olympic swimming team and yet he perished. The only assistance came from the destroyer *Mosto*, which was prevented from drawing alongside the sinking *Galilea* due to the sea conditions.

3.   The ship was in perfect working order. It was owned by Cosulich Brothers of Trieste and had recently been refitted to transport Field Marshall Graziani and his field staff to east Africa. The electric controls governing the watertight doors were up-to-date and worked too well, automatically sealing the fate of many hundreds of Alpini, the Greek prisoners and the squad of carabinieri.

4.   The wind and the rain were hitting us from the west and not vice-versa. The ship also listed strongly to the left, yet the official report sustains that the *Galilea* was hit from the right by a torpedo launched by a submarine, possibly aimed not at us, but at the *Piemonte*, a much larger ship in our convoy. No one has been able to measure the hole in the keel and doubts remain whether the ship was sunk by a torpedo or a mine.

5.   Lastly, the authors of the report expressed the belief that a modern and well-trained force would have acted with more discipline. This is also untrue. Whoever made this assertion has never been exposed to a situation where everyone is totally focused on saving oneself, where organisation disappears and every ounce of energy is dedicated to personal survival.

To conclude, a report should not be based on suppositions, but on the recollection of those who were there and survived.[14]

HITLER'S SISTER

AFTER TWO DAYS they finally gave us some clothes but when we asked what was happening the reply always came back as: "Wait. Be patient." The days passed and, as visiting authorities continued to promise everything and accomplish nothing, resentment started to build. With two of my Alpini I went to a wine shop and commandeered a small barrel of wine. I wrote out a note saying: "Good for 30 litres of wine. Signed: B. Mussolini." We reasoned that someone would eventually pay. Finally we received our departure orders, to proceed by sea back to Patras and join the rest of the Julia at Nauplia. By sea? We rebelled and Command immediately understood the absurdity of this order. We left shortly afterwards by truck, passing through Missolungi, Patras and Nauplia. On 26th April we arrived back at Udine, the capital city of the Friuli region. There, we were greeted with great warmth and emotion, all the more so since so many Alpini from this area had not come back.

Figure 12: The King of Italy reviews the Julia division at Udine in July 1942 before their departure for the Russian front

At divisional command in Udine they gave us 500 lira each to buy a new uniform. This wasn't near enough to buy the clothes and all the sundries such as mountain boots and hat. Luckily I had left my good uniform, not the combat one, with my Lucia in Carmagnola, where I went immediately.

Then, before going to visit my parents in Dresden, I made a brief trip to Rome, to visit Rosanna Mottola and my aunt Zia Emma. I was wearing my new uniform with the stripes of 1st Lieut, my promotion having arrived in January 1942.

At one point, I was sitting at a café on Via Veneto, when I heard some people commenting on the sinking of the *Galilea* and ridiculing what had happened. I jumped to my feet, furious, and told them and the others in the café to stop talking rubbish. You could have heard a pin drop. Even with friends, recounting the sinking disturbed me. No one could understand what we had been through or comprehend that this nightmare continued to plague me night and day. It is still with me today, many decades later.

I arrived in Dresden a few days later. My sister Gloria, in her eccentric way, had written to me: "Too bad, here in Kenya the cathedral has been marvellously prepared for the funeral of the Duca d'Aosta[15]. Had you departed us for good, you would have enjoyed the same draperies and profusion of flowers." "Sure, that may be true", I thought, "but, for crying out loud, I would prefer to postpone the event."

In Germany, everything was concentrated on the war effort, with everyone making sacrifices to help the Wehrmacht to reach victory. This was a surprising contrast to what I had seen in Italy, where. though prices might have been higher, people seemed to be able to ignore that we were fighting on various fronts.

In Dresden, my father introduced me to a visitor, whom we referred to as "Frau Mein Bruder". This was Adolf Hitler's sister. Every week, she came to see us and stayed for a meal. In conversation, she repeatedly said: "Mein Bruder sagt..." ("my brother says..."). She was a simple, good woman, who did not throw her weight around because of her family connection to the Fuhrer. I had the insight that Mussolini and Hitler were alike; both had come from families of humble origins but neither had feathered their nests, even though they could have had anything they desired. Who was this Frau Mein Bruder who, almost incognito, visited us weekly so she could eat better? And who was Rachele Mussolini (Mussolini's wife) who preferred to live in her farmhouse in Romagna rather that in a Roman palace?

My father got a further 15 days' leave for me and introduced me to some interesting and influential people. There was Dr Volmann, president of Zeiss Ikon, who, having heard of my surviving the shipwreck and my Leica getting wet, offered me a new camera, even though the old one still worked well. There was also the family of Graf Von Lederbur, who invited me to one of their seven castles in Silesia to hunt deer. The count's son was lost, missing in action, on the Russian front.[16]

In the centre of Dresden I noticed groups of 30 to 40 people working on the roads, in clothes with black and white stripes. They were POWs who, after their day's work, returned to the *lager* for the night. My father and I received permission to visit this *lager*, situated an hour's drive from Dresden. It had an enormous number of prisoners, who appeared to be decently housed and could circulate freely within the camp. Unfortunately, we could not understand the replies to our questions, as the prisoners spoke mainly Russian or Polish. The guards told us they were paid for their work with extra bread and tobacco and had all they needed, including medical assistance. I asked myself how it could be possible that the population was on food rations, while the prisoners appeared to be living normally. And yet, that is what we witnessed.

5: RUSSIA

THE EASTERN FRONT

SINCE OUR RETURN to Udine in April 1942 rumours were persistent that war operations were about to be extended and that the Julia division was again to be deployed, this time to the Russian front. Today, many people remain mystified as to why Germany, whose armies were already greatly extended across Europe and north Africa, elected to go against the Soviet Union as well. Again, the reader should bear in mind the information and the conditions pertaining at the time.

The Soviet Union was at its weakest. Stalin's purges had decapitated the army of many of its most independent and effective officers. Agriculture had yet to fully recover from the forced collectivisation that had proved such a catastrophe in the mid- to late 1920s, with the ensuing resentment kept at bay only by terror. In addition, the forces of the Axis had achieved great superiority over the Allies in terms of training and equipment, as both Italy and Germany had been able to test them in Spain during the Civil War, and Japan during the offensive against China in 1937. Germany was convinced that a last push would bring the Soviet Union to its knees, and open the way to the oil reserves of the Caucasus and ultimately the Suez Canal, bringing a mortal blow to the British Empire.

My friend Minini wrote to me in Dresden, saying that the survivors of the *Galilea* were being prevented from rejoining their old units. An order had been issued, stating that we survivors had already more than done our duty, in Albania, Greece and in being shipwrecked. In addition, an international understanding had it that those who had survived a sinking ship would not be sent back to the front line. The *Galilea's* survivors were therefore ordered to remain in Italy to preside over home territory. On 8th May I returned to Friuli and met some of my Alpini who were unhappy to be restricted to homeland duties. We all went together to visit Gen Ricagno, commandant of the Julia division and we volunteered to leave for the Russian front. The general was moved and ordered that we should be reintegrated into our old units. I therefore rejoined my old battalion and took charge of the mortar platoon once more. The officer commanding the Gemona was clearly annoyed at this intervention, but it was tough luck for him. We volunteers went to Tarcento to celebrate the event appropriately.

In Udine, on 20th June 1942 the whole division was inspected by HM the King of Italy. The Julia's flag was decorated with the Medaglia d'Oro, in acknowledgement of sacrifices during the Greek campaign. I spent my last five days' leave with my Lucia, on the sea near Genoa, a brief and beautiful few days. I could have never guessed it was to be the last time we spent together.

By the 8th August we were already en route. We left Italy in four trains, with the soldiers in cattle carriages, officers in second class and a whole carriage for the toilets. We reached Halle, where my family, alerted by telegram, briefly joined me to say farewell at the station. I had a 1:500,000 scale map of southern Russia and Lieut-Col Dall'Armi, commanding the Gemona, asked my father to forward another ten to him, as they were not available in Italy at that time.

We reached Warsaw in Poland and saw women and old men working at the station, each wearing a large yellow star on the chest and sleeve. Apparently they were Jews. I had not noticed them in Dresden or Frankfurt. We gave them bread and fruit, without paying attention to the German guards who yelled and made a great fuss around us. Why were there so many guards? It was the first time I had seen the yellow stars, of which much would be said after the war.

We continued on, crossing Bielorussia, and made our way towards the Caucasus. The further east we proceeded, the more we noticed the flatness of the land and the villages destroyed by the war. The soil was incredibly rich, with coal at ground level. To refuel the locomotive all we needed to do was to shovel it up into the tender. When retreating from the Germans, the Russians had made an ingenious device which, pulled by the locomotive, uprooted the rails. The Germans, however, were quickly rebuilding the track, although now with standard European gauge, the Russians having used an 18cm wider gauge. After a four-day stop in Minsk, we passed Gomel and Kharkov, reaching Isyum on 20th August. There, to our surprise, we were told that we would no longer be deployed in the mountains of the Caucasus as part of the

German 18th Army, but that we needed to advance on foot, by forced march, into the flat expanse of the Ukraine, towards the river Don. Again on foot, as in Albania and in Greece – how could a modern army be so disorganised?

We later realised that our presence in Russia was a "gesture of friendly participation" on the part of the Italian government and Mussolini. They had offered to send a whole expeditionary corps (the Italian 8th Army, known as Corpo di Spedizione Italiano in Russia, or CSIR) of 300,000 men to the Russian front, to celebrate both nations' success in helping the Nationalists win the Spanish Civil War. The CSIR included an Alpino Army Corps, which comprised three divisions – the Julia, Tridentina and Cuneense – making a total of 60,000 men and 15,000 mules. However, the hard lessons learnt in the war against Greece had already been forgotten, so this "gesture" was launched without proper planning or organisation.

The Alpino Army Corps was formed of those who had specialised in mountain warfare. They had been recruited from a limited section of the population and were more costly to train. The news of our new destination was greeted with great worry and disappointment by us all, especially the senior officers. The decision was to prove a costly error, both for us and the Germans. It was due to the strategy of the German high command in attempting to outflank the Russian armies from the south, to occupy Stalingrad and then turn northwards towards Moscow. The error in deploying us on a vast plain without mechanised transport was compounded by a lack of adequate armament and clothing. But those were the orders.

I should describe the clothing and weaponry of the Alpino Corps in Russia, comparing it to our German ally and to the Soviet enemy, which was fighting on home territory. The Alpino clothing comprised: a short cape to the knee, as we had in Albania, but which in the winter of 1942 was substituted for a heavy linen overcoat, lined with fur for sentry duty; woollen cagoule and mittens; light or heavy leather mountain boots, rubber-soled but without hobnails (in low temperatures they caused frostbite); woollen vest; tent canvas, also for use against the rain. In contrast, the Germans (who copied the Russians) had: a heavy-duty jacket and trousers lined with fur; woollen cap or hat, with ear protection; boots lined with fur (for the Russians, felt *valenki)*; heavy mittens.

On leaving for the Russian front, every Alpino – myself included – acquired warm clothing for the severe winter awaiting us, even though there was a limit as to how much we could fit into our rucksacks.

As for firepower, both the Germans and the Russians had been provided with automatic weapons, with a clear superiority in calibre and fire rate. Our rifle, the excellent and reliable '91 model with its six-cartridge magazine, always worked, even if wet or in temperatures of minus-30 degrees. However, it had to be reloaded after every shot. In arctic temperatures, our Breda machine-guns only worked if you squeezed a few shots every 15 minutes. Also, our 3.2-tonne tanks – known as sardine tins – were totally outclassed by the Leopard or Tigre models used by the Germans, or by the Russian T-34's (34 tonnes), ten times bigger. Our only really effective weapons were our 81mm mortars and "Oto" hand-grenades. As in Albania, my 81mm mortars wreaked carnage in Russia too.

To the Don

WE SET OFF FROM Isyum heading east, each of us with his own rucksack. The weather was good. The terrain was undulating, with sparse woods interspersed with fields of sunflowers and wheat. Roads were few, none were asphalted and, to our surprise, they were 40 to 50 metres wide, with signs placed by the Germans to indicate villages. It was impossible to use these roads in the rain, as we quickly become mired in mud. In all of Ukraine we hardly found a stone, nothing but sand and clay. The few stones we found were flint, good for our cigarette lighters.

The march continued and we covered between 20 and 25 kilometres every day, without knowing our precise destination. After well over 100km, we stopped for four days at the town of Rowenki. In my mess tin I cooked a chicken I had caught as we entered the town. I've never eaten a tastier one, and still remember the flavour after 60 years. In the few villages we passed through we did not see many people, usually only women and children. They were reasonably well nourished but dressed in rough clothing, as the poor dress. You could see that they had suffered considerably, first under the Communist regime, then under the abuses of the German occupation. With us present, the situation changed and a relationship of cordiality and mutual assistance started to develop.

In crossing Ukraine, we came to be acquainted with a central element of Russian housing, the *isba*. This was a country cottage, built of wood, square and with a single floor about a metre off the ground. Between the ground and the floor an enclosed space was used to store vegetables and small farm animals. The walls were planks of wood loosely fitted together and plastered with mud and straw, with the roof also made of compressed straw. These materials and how the *isba* was built combined to maintain a constant and comfortable temperature indoors of about 20 degrees centigrade, even if the outside temperature fell to minus-40. The windows were small and double-glazed with external shutters, one of which could be opened.

Figure 13: On forced march from Isyum to the River Don in August/September 1942

The Russians did not burn wood in their stoves, but bricks of straw mixed with manure, roughly 25 x 35cm, and 5cm thick.

When lit, there was no flame, but the bricks generated lasting and intense heat, more effective than wood or charcoal. They were also difficult to put out, even in the rain. Their only drawback was that, in burning, they gave off a marked smell of manure or rotten fish.

Another feature of the *isba* was the lice. A Russian proverb said that every house has its lice. This was true – they were everywhere, in the straw embedded in the walls, in the gaps between floorboards, or hidden in the ceiling. No chemical agent could kill them so they were the constant companions of every Russian who, as a result, washed often, were very clean and scrubbed their houses enthusiastically.

The *isba* had no running water, so it had to be carried from the nearest well and the toilet was outdoors. It consisted of a basic wooden cabin usually situated in the vegetable patch.

Entrance to an *isba* was via wooden steps, through two doors, the second of which was lined. This led to the only room, in the middle of which was a large stove, for cooking and heating. Bedding was on shelves around and above the stove. Normally a table had chairs or stools around it, while in a corner sat a few family photographs and the family icon. Despite Soviet policy, in the Ukraine religion was still strongly felt.

From Rowenki we continued eastwards. But those daily 20km hikes started to weigh on us and, towards the end, we were only covering about 15km a day. At that point the rucksacks were loaded on to trucks, and each man continued with his tactical backpack. As far as I was concerned, I still felt in good shape and continued the march with my full rucksack. Just 10km before Rossoch, our destination and HQ of the Alpine Army Corps, we were picked up by trucks so that everybody seeing us arrive would think we were a motorized deployment. It was bare-faced hypocrisy, but also an insult by our general command, mocking us as they had already done in Albania and Greece. But we needed to hurry, as the 284th German Division had to head south, towards Stalingrad, leaving our division to man a front line of about 30km on the Don. Across the river were numerous Russian divisions so 30km for our single division – 13,000 men – was a tall order!

Finally, on 19th September we reached the Don and the front line, near a cluster of *isbe* called Dukowoje. Only hours later we received the order to move again a few kilometres north, to Semeiki. This instruction annoyed me, as we had started to make camp under a windmill, with a beautiful view over the Don. At last, in reaching Semeiki, our long march was over.

At that point, the Don was about 70 metres wide. The left bank on the Russian side was flat, whereas our bank was high, giving us considerable tactical advantage. The weather was still good. Losing no time, we started to organise ourselves for a prolonged stay, aware that winter would not be far away.

Our hopes that the Germans would have made this natural defensive position stronger and more comfortable were not realised. The position was not logically set out, no approaches were protected from enemy fire, no supply depots were covered and logistical structures were absent. We deduced that this sector of the front had remained calm throughout the summer. So why hadn't our allies used the long break to fortify the line? We were comforted by the fact that the Soviet air force was not around, except for the odd reconnaissance plane. In addition, the enemy's spirit was low – the many deserters described a lack of enthusiasm among the population for this war. In addition, the presence of German armoured units behind us was a further positive factor, as they would have covered us in case of attack.

The enemy across the river had not reached a high operational level but, if in our area the Russians remained invisible by day, they became very active at night.

The possibility of having to remain here for the winter made us determined to fortify our line defensively, even though our units were stretched out. After initially receiving a number of orders to position and reposition gun emplacements and bunkers, by the end of October we were able to start work in earnest, with my Alpini of the mortar platoon achieving near miracles. In a large depression parallel to the Don, we dug a bunker for 20 men, four metres deep. The roof was made of alternate layers of timber, earth and straw, so as to absorb shelling. A smaller bunker was dug for me, with a fireplace and chimney, which I furnished with a camp bed and small table and chair we had found in no-man's land. That's where all the timber used in building our position had also been found.

Of the 20 mortars allocated to my unit, we only retained four in the immediate vicinity of the large bunker. The others, with their teams, were detached much further away, to preside over as much of the front line as possible. One of these teams was led by Papinutti, now a sergeant. In no-man's land we found other items of greater interest, such as seven chickens. Only three survived the journey back to our lines, the others having ended up in our pot. Capturing three pigs on the riverbank and transporting them back to our position was more challenging because of all the noise they made. We baptised them as Don, Volga and Donetz.

We had little wine and had to drink boiled water normally but, somehow, some wine did materialise. I feared for our three pigs, as inspections might reveal their presence and make other units envious. So we built a superb little bunker for them, with an efficient drainage system. One evening we gathered in the large bunker, and decided that Volga and Don would eventually be given to the detached mortar teams, while we kept little Donetz. But how would we prepare him: roasted on the spit? Served with risotto? Stewed? Decisions…

Our daily food rations, which punctually reached us by mule, were not bad and quite sufficient, as was the tobacco. But the Alpini are special: our area was full of mice that subsisted on grain and one of us had a clever idea. "*Sior Tenente*, look, just try this," he said, offering me what seemed like two small birds cooked in butter. But no, they were mice. They were delicious and much better than birds that eat worms.

With the end of October the cold started to intensify. At the same time we noticed that the Russians had considerably increased their activity, with artillery fire and raids on our positions. The German armoured units to our rear were suddenly moved south, perhaps because of the growing concentration of effort needed to overcome the enemy's resistance at Stalingrad. We already realised that winter was the Russians best ally and knew that, as soon as the ice on the river was thick enough, their tanks would easily cross the Don. We still had many deserters coming to us, although some were certainly ready to cross back to their own lines and reveal the true state of our defences and fire-power. We started to experience our first casualties. According to Fra' Generoso, a colleague lieutenant had died after stepping on a mine.

The cold weather affected our three pigs and they caught a chill. But the Alpino who had built their bunker was also an expert pig man and decided that what they needed was a hot bath. This they were duly given, while little Donetz, to whom we were especially attached, was also given massages. That cured the problem and my pig man received an extra ration of wine.

One night, my private little bunker caught fire and I had to evacuate. One of the layers of straw between earth and timber, through which the chimney reached the surface, had ignited in the heat. I transferred to the main bunker, where my Alpini had also managed to make some fresh white bread from the wheat that grew abundantly in the area. The wheat grains were ground in a helmet and an Alpino even produced some yeast.

We reached November and things started to heat up. In front of our position, in the middle of the Don, was the little island of Semeiki. From our observation point on the riverbank we had never noticed any activity in daytime, but by night the island had become much noisier. The Russians were preparing something and I repeatedly warned command, but with no result. I decided to take matters into my own hands.

I had a mortar hidden about 100 metres from the island and had our supply of high-power mortar bombs – equivalent to 155mm artillery shells – carried there. I considered my decision again and concluded that it could only prove positive. One night, we fired all the bombs on to the island. Shouts and mayhem followed. In the morning, we saw that it had been destroyed. To my amazement, instead of receiving a commendation for eliminating an advanced enemy position threatening our line, I got a reproach from my Col Dall'Armi: "Don't you realise, *Tenente*, that you have used up your allocation of a type of ammunition that is scarce? You should have waited for permission before taking action." It was yet another disagreement with my command in which, being the subordinate officer, I obviously had to be in the wrong.

GARRISON DUTY

BECAUSE OF THIS EPISODE, and perhaps one or two other instances where my independence of spirit had ruffled feathers, I received the order from Col Dall'Armi to leave the Gemona battalion and join our 28th Supply Unit in Oligowatka, about 20km away from the front line. After the war, it dawned on me that the colonel's decision may also have been influenced by my father, who I realise had remained in contact with him. I was not allowed to take any weapons with me, not even my pistol. Farewell,

Gemona. If leaving the front was welcome for some, for me it was a real punishment.

Before leaving my Alpini, we sacrificed our little Donetz. The piglet was transformed into a fabulous roast that we all savoured. After that I collected my rucksack and left for Saprina, where the regiment was based. Before leaving, my Alpini gave me a beautiful icon, found God knows where, which I packed in my rucksack. I reached Saprina late in the night, after a terrible journey. The truck repeatedly crushed the thin ice and got bogged down in mud. I spent the rest of the night in an *isba* and donated the icon to the old woman who lived there with her three children. She embraced me with tears in her eyes; the Germans had taken everything they owned, even their sacred images. While waiting for transportation to Oligowatka, I spent two days in Rossoch, where our Army HQ was based. I noticed that the population seemed well fed.

There was, however, also a sense of nervousness in the air. From the end of that 1942 summer, the United States and Britain had been sending massive convoys of weapons, ammunition and transport to the Soviet Union, whose industry was also beginning to achieve high levels of production. In addition, the news concerning the German 6th Army at Stalingrad was not good, with Von Paulus having to receive reinforcements initially intended for our sector. We also heard rumours that our two divisions on the Don were facing two Soviet armies – with 125 battalions, 750 tanks and 300 anti-tank guns.

I arrived at Oligowatka on a sleigh and, on reaching the 28th Supply Unit, I received my new orders from the captain. I was ordered to take responsibility for an area 18km away that had just been vacated by the Germans. The accompanying instructions were worrying:

- The area I was to preside over was totally isolated. The only contact with command would consist of the daily delivery of food and mail.
- I would be allocated 40 Alpini, two machine-guns, a case of hand-grenades and a little ammunition.
- We needed to remain vigilant, as the departing Germans had suffered severe casualties due to the numerous partisans in the area, some of whom had arrived by parachute.

- I was encouraged to do my best to ingratiate ourselves with the locals, as we would not receive additional supplies or reinforcements.

I was surprised that our command would even consider sending a unit with scarce armaments and supplies into an area with confirmed enemy activity. Wasting no time, I sent a written request, marked "private and confidential", to Col Cimolino of the 8th Regiment, stating that since 1940 I had always been on the front line and that I wanted to rejoin it as a volunteer. The eventual reply praised my request and confirmed that I would be recalled to the front line sometime in December. It even offered me a choice between joining the Tolmezzo or the Cividale battalions, although no longer the Gemona.

Before leaving Oligowatka, I acquired a pair of magnificent white felt *valenki* (boots) and a Walther P38 pistol. I found it superior to our Berettas and it used the same 9mm ammunition. I left with 35 Alpini on sleighs pulled by mules, fully equipped for the Russian winter: in addition to the *valenki* I also had a fur jacket and hat, and thick woollen underwear. The only annoying element was my beard and long moustache, which froze in the cold weather and made it difficult to open my mouth.

The area assigned to me covered seven *kolkhoz* (collective farm) of which the most important was Krasnij Partizan. I had 40 Alpini at my disposal, armed with two machine-guns. With them I had to control more than 400 hectares of birch forest and fields with potatoes, wheat and sunflowers. I settled myself, as best I could, at Krasnji Partizan with its 600 Russian inhabitants.

I soon discovered an *isba* that the Germans had turned into a prison, to detain locals who refused to go to work in the *valenki* factory at Oligowatka, 20 kilometres away. My first decision was to open the doors and free the prisoners – including the village priest, who had been forced by the Soviets to work as a cart-driver and had continued in this profession under the Germans. I told him that I preferred him to resume his old position. To celebrate the event, I removed the curfew imposed on the seven *kolkhoz*. The population was invited to join us at the local command post in the former school at four in the afternoon with their balalaikas. Accompanied by our accordion player, we would all dance together. This caused general amazement and enthusiasm among the population, particularly the priest, who returned to his family.

Everyone was overjoyed that the Italians had arrived to replace the Germans.

A little later, on the invitation of the priest, I visited him at his *isba* since he wanted to teach me how to drink vodka – which he did. I learnt, while eating *kasha*, an oat-based gruel with pieces of lard, how to drink a brimful glass of vodka in one go, and then another. "Never sip it!" I was told. The priest, and the rest of his large family all became my friends. I often visited to practice my new skill.

While reconnoitring the area on a small sleigh pulled by a mule, I managed to contact our somewhat distant cavalry unit. The commander was horrified by our lack of weapons. He gave me a precision, automatic Russian rifle – a Tokarev STV-40 – with ammunition and, for the troop, some grenades and rifle bullets. I placed great faith in my STV but discarded it a few days later when, aiming at a hare in the forest, the weapon did not fire. It had jammed due to the cold. What a disappointment.

I wrote home: "I wouldn't mind being killed in the front line with a bullet or a grenade but the thought of dying here, in such a moronic way, is more than I can bear."

Having taken over from the Germans, I kept up only one important duty inherited from them – every week I went to a nearby *isba* to take a bath. Two girls, aged 20 and 23 and both students, prepared a tin bath for me in their small living room. They helped me to undress, poured hot or cold water over me as requested, and washed me with soap (which I then left them as a present). I did not let them dry me as this would have been excessive, but they did wash my linen for me. I also found a beautiful girl to teach me Russian. I had every intention of learning it well and, in fact, soon managed a reasonable number of phrases. She was a school-teacher from Kiev and I could hardly ask for anything better.

Every evening I ate a delicious dinner with the troop at four o'clock. I say evening, since the sun set at two, having risen at 10 in the morning. After dinner, the mess room was open for dancing. The Ukrainian police force garrisoned with us was made up of around 20 lads between the ages of 14 and 16. They ate with us. They did not take orders from me, but I protected them and they counted on our food.

One December morning, one of the teenage policemen came to see me accompanied by the head *starosta* (local elder), to inform me that the body of a naked, decapitated man had been found in the forest near a village about a kilometre away. I left immediately for the wood and discovered that it was a young man, with clear signs that he had been bound and beaten. He had a large wound on one leg. We never found the head, but it had evidently been removed with a heavy dull instrument since some teeth had fallen out from the force of the impact and were found on the remaining part of the neck. He was definitely a Russian, which could be deduced from the fact that his fingers were blackened by the local *mahorka* tobacco, which only the Russians smoked. The body was frozen hard as stone and, as the sun was already setting, we left him there for the night. We brought him back to the empty village prison the next day so that he could be identified. However, he remained an enigma and the questions of who he was or why he had died in such a brutal manner were never answered. In the snow surrounding the body I found some tracks with traces of *valenki* and rifle butts. It was probably the partisans who had killed one of their own.

In this less-than-reassuring environment, it was my duty to keep my Alpini as calm as possible and to keep up their morale. This was no easy task, particularly since I was hardly at ease myself. We suffered from a lack of men and weapons and were cut off from the rest of the world. We also needed to be on our guard 24 hours a day. I ordered my men to be as friendly as possible with the population, although, in reality, this was already happening. Most of the men had already found themselves a girlfriend in the villages.

Another unexpected event occurred. One of the patrols, together with a few of the policemen, captured a partisan, called Ivan, in the woods. Ivan was 24, emaciated, starving and extremely dirty. Above all, he was convinced that, as a partisan, he was going to be shot. He was dragged before me and the interpreter informed me that he had lost his unit in the forest a few days ago. What would be the best and most prudent tactic, I asked myself? I made him understand that he had nothing to fear from us and ordered that he be given a good hot shower, washed, shaved and provided with some of our clothes. He was, however, allowed to keep his *ushanka* (fur hat with ear flaps).

When he was brought back before me he had become a different man, and, with a meal inside him, he seemed a normal person again. In order to keep an eye on him, I made him my attendant and was amazed by the devotion he showed me. He had expected to be tried and shot so he felt he owed me his life. Ivan attended me until I left the garrisoned area and returned to the front on the Don. On that day, with a hug and, on his request, a blessing, I set him free and never saw him again.

This was a king's life, comfortable but potentially even more dangerous than the front line. At least there I knew where the bullets were likely to arrive from. The idyll came to an end on the morning of 19th December 1942, when I received the order to rejoin the front line.

Before leaving, to please the girls but also for personal comfort, I shaved beard and moustache. From appearing very old I regained the features of a young man. The girls approved: "*Sicias ocien Kharasho!* (That is much better!)" they said.

QUOTA CIVIDALE

I LEFT KRASNIJ PARTISAN alone and when I reached Oligowatka I was provided with a sleigh and an Alpino. We set off to rejoin the front line. The journey took an incredible 17 days, on sleigh and on foot, with the temperature dropping to between 35 and 40 degrees below zero. We travelled to army command in Rossoch and from there to Kureni, where my destination was finally confirmed to be with the Cividale battalion. One of the three battalions in the 8th Alpino regiment – the others being the Gemona and Tolmezzo – the Cividale was still deployed on the Don at Novo Kalitwa, the furthermost position to the east.

On our way to the front line, I started to hear deeply demoralising news. Not only were the Germans having little success further south at Stalingrad, but the Soviets had launched a formidable offensive in the area occupied by our units. And they were supported by tanks and artillery.

On our way, we saw new units of the Vicenza division, just arrived from Italy. These were badly put together from diverse army corps, disorganised, untrained and still in summer uniform. The new division also had no artillery. We were stunned and asked ourselves how it was possible to send into combat a large unit in such a desperate state. In war, if you do not have the means to put together an effective fighting force, you wait until you are able to do so. We mockingly called the new unit Divisione Brambilla (equivalent to the Mickey Mouse division).

Destruction and abundant traces of fighting were also evident. I saw German and Italian corpses and noted that some of German dead had been castrated. From abandoned supply depots I filled my rucksack with food and equipment, and found a new *fufaika*, a heavy winter jacket. The journey proved long and tortuous, but I finally reached the Cividale on the front line on 5th January 1943.

When I arrived at the tent of Lieut-Col Zacchi, who had also been my commanding officer and friend in Albania, I saw Capt Magnani, a good friend who was also with me in Albania. He greeted me warmly, adding: "Look here, these are the dead from yesterday and today". He pointed to about 15 corpses covered with ground sheets. It was about 3pm and it was already getting dark. That day, divisional command notified me of my promotion to captain, with effect from 15th January.

I entered the tent, barely illuminated by a lit tin of anti-frostbite fat, and saluted Lieut-Col Zacchi, who had just learned that he had lost another officer. He seemed depressed. "Another one! Now they have nailed Capt Chiaradia as well. You, Ferrante, go immediately to the Quota and take over 20th Company. There are only about two dozen men left but, with luck, reinforcements should be on the way". Poor Cividale and poor Zacchi, I thought. However, both Zacchi and Magnani survived the war without a scratch, becoming POWs. They were repatriated after the war. I met them both again at Soviet prison camp NKVD 160, at Suzdal.

The Quota (position at 176m elevation) at Nova Kalitwa merits a few words. It had previously been presided over by a unit of the XXIV German Army Corps. They had called it Quota Signal, because of a trigonometric reference point on the top. During their offensive, the Russians overran the German defence and our Julia division was called upon to regain it, a feat which it achieved. We handed it back to the Germans. This occurred a second time, then a third. After that, the Julia retained it, using the Cividale battalion. Although exhausted by the fighting and the cold, we remained to preside over this position, so it was renamed the Quota Cividale.

We held on by the skin of our teeth, but I noticed by observing the immediate area that losses by the Soviets were more than 10 times ours. Their continuous attacks were assisted by artillery fire and by Katyusha multiple-rocket launchers, which caused great noise but comparatively few casualties. I could clearly see the enemy advancing in line, as they did during the Napoleonic wars. Their officers and commissars took up the rear, and remorselessly shot any who hesitated. It gave me an eerie feeling.

Figure 14: In position on the Don, September 1942

In the few moments of respite, I had to reorganize and encourage our force, helped by the only other officer who had survived, Lieut Giovannella. I still remember the body of one of our Alpini, lying on the little snow left, with a Russian bayonet stuck in his stomach. Among the many Soviet dead, we found quite a few women. Their hair had been shaved off and they were identical to the men. The difference only became apparent when we took their tags and realised they had breasts. We mowed down these poor people in their hundreds until we exhausted all our ammunition.

I know the Russians never provided figures regarding how many of their soldiers died in our area. Many years after the end of the war, I was informed that today a stone slab has been placed on the Quota, in remembrance of the heavy loss of Russian life. No names or figures are mentioned, however.

At the time, I was surprised to see that the Soviets neglected to collect their wounded, leaving them to freeze to death. We painfully learnt later as POWs that the mentality of poor Russians was suffused with fatalism. Evidence came in the enormous number of people conscripted to fight the invader. They were sent to their slaughter and were afraid of us but even more of the *Politruk* (political commissar). Rarely was one of their wounded assisted, especially in the frigid winter. The cold numbed the pain in any case. Their dead were left on the ground, as also ours would later be too. "They are good manure," the Russians said. Today, any criticism is useless. Even if difficult, we must try to understand their mentality and the situation we all found ourselves in.

The fighting on the Quota Cividale was intense and constant. From 6th to the 16th of January, the day when I was wounded, no respite came. We were so few that even the men with second-degree frostbite had to stay on (with third-degree you have gangrene and must be hospitalised). We took the gloves and the *valenki* off the dead to help the living.

One moonless night I decided to reconnoitre the area between the two lines and asked Cpl Borgobello to come with me. We were both in white camouflage, which was not very effective as the snow had almost entirely disappeared under artillery shelling. Borgobello also had severe frostbite.

Not far from our line facing the enemy we saw in a dugout a 15mm Russian anti-tank rifle, two metres long. To my surprise it seemed abandoned so we both shouldered it and started to return to our lines. Suddenly I realised that we also needed its ammunition so I discharged my Verey pistol to illuminate the area. At that moment we saw two Russians, also in white camouflage, but they were running away. However, we also needed to return immediately as the enemy was now aware of our incursion. It is only then that I remembered that we no longer had the correct password – which was changed every half hour because of the dangerous circumstances. Also, because of the freezing weather, we had given orders for a few machine-gun rounds to be fired off every 15 minutes, to keep them in working order. Arriving near our lines, I yelled as loudly as I could: "This is Lieut Ferrante, let us pass." To my relief, nobody shot at us.

The fighting intensified. One afternoon, exhausted by the lack of sleep, I dropped in the snow where I stood and fell asleep. I was alone. Suddenly, I was awoken by a field mouse which, thinking me dead, had bitten my ring finger through the thick glove. It was nothing, but to have been taken for dead affected me deeply. In addition, we had fried and eaten those field mice. My longing for sleep vanished.

Events then overtook us. The Soviet offensive had continued to increase, placing ever-increasing pressure on the overstretched units on the Don front. This effort had been helped by a massive supply effort from the US which, throughout 1942, had supplied its Soviet ally with thousands of tanks, trucks and ammunition, in addition to all the materiel needed to sustain the offensive. In the second week of January, the sectors held by the Romanian Army (to our south) and by the Germans and Norwegians (to our north) gave way. Russian motorised divisions streamed through, followed by infantry. The enemy columns reached a depth of about 300km, before starting a giant pincer movement to mop up surviving German, Italian and allied units.

We on the Quota Cividale near Novo Kalitwa, the position furthest east on the front, knew nothing of all this. We had pushed back attack after attack but held on to our positions, as had the whole of our sector, manned by the Alpino Corps and a number of German and Romanian units. Our success was perhaps also due to all the work carried out to entrench ourselves before the soil froze.

Suddenly, however, this advantage evaporated, as we were confronted with the danger of encirclement. On 16th January, I received the order to disengage my company at 24hr and withdraw to the second line behind us. Then I realised that the German field artillery position immediately behind us, commanded by an Oberleutnant, was evacuating its pieces of artillery. "What's this?" I asked him. He replied that it was nothing to do with us and that he was only obeying orders. I started to get angry, as we needed the cover of their guns. I asked him to remain where he was. I added that I was in charge of the sector, so I was his senior and would give him precisely three minutes to bring back his pieces. Failing that, I would shoot him on the spot. I extracted my pistol. I felt calm and would have shot him without hesitation. He realised this and within seconds I saw the pieces of artillery returning.

As this was unfolding, a sharp increase of artillery fire gave us warning of another large-scale Russian attack. I began quickly to reorganise my limited resources when I saw a corporal arriving with canteens full of grappa, intended to revitalise the men before the attack. He was drunk though as, on his way up to our position, he had drunk a lot of the liquor destined for his companions. Here again I was tempted to shoot him on the spot, but I calmed down on realising that his chances of survival in the coming battle were nil.

At the beginning of the afternoon I realised that the telephone line with command had been interrupted. We were all at our combat positions, so I decided to go forward myself to locate the broken wire, repair it and re-establish communication. I found the fault and repaired it, but suddenly noticed a large Russian tank about 800m away. Its gun was pointing in our direction. At that moment something like large fireworks exploded above me. I felt a strong blow to the head and fell. I vaguely remember being loaded on to a stretcher on two skis and hearing a medical officer, perhaps Lieut Marzuttin, saying: "It's probably nothing too serious, I'll give him an anti-tetanus jab..." I lost consciousness. For me, that was the end of the fighting.

6: PRISONER

COMBATANT TO PRISONER

A FTER BEING WOUNDED on the Quota Cividale, I can only remember fleeting and confused moments. I stopped being a combatant and the Italian authorities listed me as missing in action. For those who saw me, I seemed "dead" or "dying". I was apparently put on a large sleigh that served as a field ambulance. With me was my orderly, who carried a one-litre canteen full of grappa, from which he fed me sips. I am told that I emptied the canteen. Showing no further signs of life, my white fur boots and heavy gloves were taken, the inevitable bequest of the dead for the living.

Many years later, I asked survivors who were with me at the time to write to me with their recollections of these events. Gen Sensale, then a 2nd Lieut with the Gemona battalion, wrote to me, confirming that:

"The Gemona was retreating and I was closing in on the column when we came across an abandoned sleigh-ambulance on its side. I thought I heard the whimpering of a dog and, opening its door, I saw a person in white camouflage with a lieutenant's stripes, slumped and covered in blood. There was an explosion and soon after a German car appeared, its occupants having just blown up the ice on the Kalitwa river to slow down the Soviet advance. I signalled the car to stop and, with my rudimentary German, said: "Gibt es hier ein verwundete Italienische Offizier" (We have a wounded Italian officer here). The driver got out of the car, muttering under his breath. Together, we pulled this wounded officer from the ambulance and it was then that I recognised Ferrante. I tried to speak to him, but received no answer. I did not insist further, as the Krauts were willing to take him to the Krankenhaus (hospital) and we were all in a hurry, they to clear the area and

I to rejoin our column. We put him lying down on the knees of the three passengers on the back seat. "Danke schon", I said. "Leben Sie woll", they replied and the car sped away. Because of all the blood in the throat area, I frankly did not expect him to survive.

But thank God, that was not to be and, about a year later in POW camp 160, at Suzdal, I heard that a new Italian officer, Lieut Ferrante of the Julia division, had arrived. He was walking unsteadily with the help of two sticks and I ran up to him, asking what happened when he had first reached the hospital. His reply was unclear, partly because all the other POWs were pressing him with questions. I had the impression that he had still not totally recovered his mental faculties. A few days later I told him how I had left him with the Germans to take him to the field hospital. His only reply was: "Maybe it was the Germans who stole my boots…"

I came to on an operating table where they wanted to give another anti-tetanus jab. I refused it. I saw Fra' Generoso there, who had been with me in Albania, but he quickly disappeared as the hospital went up in flames. One of my colleagues, I think it was Giovannella, loaded me on his back and placed me on an open truck. I was evacuated to the hospital in Podgornoje. By the time I reached the hospital, without gloves or boots, I was showing no signs of life. It was assumed I had died of cold and, as the temperature was minus-40, I was stacked with other bodies – like sardines – on one of the piles of corpses at the entrance.

Luckily, Doctor Volterrani, who was managing the hospital, happened to be passing by when he head a voice saying: "I'm an officer, get me out of here!" They extracted me from the pile of bodies and put me in a large hall. The next thing I remember was waking up days later, I think it was on the 24th, as I felt my watchstrap being undone. I stared at a beautiful girl bending over me. *"Davaj Ciassi"* (give me your watch), she was saying. She wore a strange uniform and two men with Alsatian dogs were standing behind her, wearing the same uniform. They were Russian partisans.

The Soviet army had broken through and the partisans were occupying the hospital.

I do not remember too much about Podgornoje. I know that our Army Corps had bread ovens there, bread that was distributed to us but also to the local population, who liked us as a result. The hospital was one of the few buildings in brick, as it had been the local school. Together with Doctor Volterrani, who became a good friend, I remember Capt Givanni, wounded in both legs, Camino who had frostbite to a foot and Lieut Boero. Volterrani placed Givanni and me, who were in the worst shape, in his room. As the Russians had taken all the drugs and medical equipment, Volterrani washed my head wound with permanganate and he was surprised to see that I was able to insert my thumb into the wound, which produced copious pus. As for Lieut Boero, he was a medical student but proved to be worthless. Volterrani forbade him to treat me or Givanni, whose legs were full of mortar shrapnel.

I was weak and unable to stand. On top of everything else, the shrapnel had destroyed my inner ear, which caused me severe vertigo. The shrapnel had also broken my left jaw and I could only suck, rather than chew. In any event there was no food, only a few frozen, blackened potatoes overlooked by pigs. Someone would slice them and put them on the stove next to my cot, after which they were distributed to us. I only received two or three slices a day and, as I could not chew, kept them in my mouth for a long time before swallowing them. Delicious. Fortunately I was not hungry, in contrast to Givanni, who complained at length of the shrapnel in his legs and his empty stomach. I could not defecate, which made Volterrani angry. Finally, one day I crawled nearly 20 metres to the latrine – what a trip those few metres – squatted near a pile of shit and put Volterrani's mind at ease. Fortunately, due to the intense cold, everything was completely frozen.

Still in the latrine, under the broken window a pile of soiled bandages lay outside. Over the next few days, I extracted the least dirty ones with a stick and, boiled in snow water, I was able to re-use them to bandage my head. I also had frostbite in both my feet and my toes had turned black. Volterrani informed me that if they did not register improvement, especially those on the right foot, he would have to amputate them. With a Gillette blade or nail scissors, the only surgical implements he had left. And without anaesthetic. I was terrified that Boero would be called to operate. Over time, however, my toes turned from black to red, and finally pink. I only lost my toenails. My toes were painful for some time though and Volterrani jokingly threatened to squeeze them.

Doctor Volterrani, a good man, came from Sarteano, near Siena in Tuscany, where he had qualified as a gynaecologist.

Unmarried, atheist, anti-fascist, anti-communist, anarchic, he had a spontaneous character and had mastered the most incredible repertoire of curses and swear words, with which he generously peppered his conversation. With the evacuation of our forces fleeing the Soviet offensive, he was designated to remain behind to take care of the wounded, being the youngest doctor in the hospital. Years later, we met back in Italy and he greatly enjoyed explaining to those present how he had fished me "out of that heap of corpses, left like sardines head-to-foot and foot-to-head, near the entrance to the hospital."

Days later, I caught fleck-typhus. Until then, I had hoped that the drug taken in Albania against amoebic dysentery would keep all parasites at bay, but it was not enough to deter lice, who infected me with this illness. The typhus caught in Podgornoje sent me into a coma which lasted about 10 days. I had vivid hallucinations and in one of my dreams I was congratulated by an obese Field Marshal Goering while climbing a mountain in southern Italy. I also dreamt that I was eating a delicious fish soup in Livorno in Tuscany, but I was also on board a ship full with water and sinking.

When I came out of the coma, I remained unable to remember who I was for several weeks, what my name was or that of my parents or my sister, with whom I was very close. For days, I tried to remember but in vain. I even lost track of the year we were in. I lost all my hair and became bald. I always felt thirsty, rather than hungry. The hole in my face emitted continuous pus and my frostbitten feet were still painful. My urine bottle became my faithful friend, but it was always full. I had difficulty finding someone to empty it for me.

CANNIBALISM

I WAS IN A BAD WAY, but conditions between January and May 1943 were terrible for all POWs. Our mortality rate was high, due to untended wounds and the Russians' fatalistic attitude that meant a dead body was useful for fertilising fields. This was compounded by their feeling that we had come to fight the Russian people and so had no right to live. However, death was mostly due to lack of food rather than lack of medical care, freezing temperatures or our captors' attitudes. Above all, hunger and thirst tormented us – we the unlucky ones who had survived the fighting, capture and the interminable *davaj* marches to the camps. Unlucky because our agony was destined to be prolonged instead of ending swiftly and with welcome.

We became only too aware of how nature had equipped the human body with incredible powers of resistance. After 10 to 14 days without food we suffered stomach cramps and physical decline... but we still survived. After about 20 days, we would become comatose, and we would become animals. In these conditions it was easy for us to lose our minds.

Cases of cannibalism occurred. Our subconscious minds were aware that food long dead was bad and so it was better to kill someone who was dying, and then to remove the brain and heart and eat them. They had a sweet flavour and, if the killing was carried out with colleagues (as always happened), there was no sense of remorse. The heart and brain were preferred because the rest of the body was so wasted that it had little nutrition. Heart and brain were parts of the body that deteriorated less as dying progressed. We suffered... but at least we were still alive.

The thirst was worse. For those who have endured it, this is the most terrible of tortures, much more subtle than hunger. The agony it causes can only be appreciated by those who have survived it. Our mouths, our tongues and our lips all swelled up. We wanted to put anything in our mouths to relieve our bodies' absolute need of liquids. We tried to drink urine, yet the body forced us to spit it out as it was so naturally repellent to the organism. We sought out moisture from drops of snow, leaves, even blood. This last was good when pure, but disgusting if it had been mixed with pus.

Muscular dystrophy, typhus fever and dysentery, also important causes of mortality, could all be fought with liquids rather than food. But the Russians gave us salted biscuits or dried salt bread to eat.

I remember that, in the first period between April and May, the diet and my general weakness caused my front teeth to become loose. In time, however, though very slowly, my gums hardened up again and I did not lose my teeth.

The length of time we could survive varied from person to person. It depended on our tenacity, our physical condition and consequent level of resistance, our personal circumstances, and our spirit which we either kept or lost. Everything was devastatingly relative but still the differences between people were the differences that sorted the survivors from those who died.

And yet, when on the front line or facing the enemy, with friends falling around me, death had no import. I gave it no thought. Only the stink of dead bodies revived feelings of physical repulsion. On all the battle fronts – Spain, Albania, Greece and Russia – death had never worried me. I had never feared it. The pain of a serious injury that might strike me at any moment was frightening, but death was not. The trauma deriving from a state of helpless prostration was more worrying.

I have only vague memories of this time. However, I have been able to obtain some information from another survivor, Prof Aldo Buogo, who was a 2nd Lieut. He wrote in answer to my request for information about those days.

Dear Ferrante,

I was also wounded on the Don River, as you were and on the same day, 16th January. I was then in command of the scouts platoon and had just managed to free Lieut Cenci and his men from encirclement. During that action, my achilles tendon had been ruptured by a Russian grenade and I was taken to the hospital in Podgornoje, where there was a great confusion of German, Romanian, Italian and Hungarian soldiers, some wounded, some not, with a background of shots and explosions of all kinds. Dr Volterrani repaired the damage to my tendon from that fucking grenade and I was left on the floor, like you. When the Russians arrived in heavy tanks around 20th January, we experienced hair-raising moments. They immediately seized all the German and more than a few Italian officers and, together with seven Finnish soldiers, took them outside and shot them in the back of the head. The bodies were left where they fell.

I was one of the lucky ones. I was wearing white camouflage and was immediately identified as a combat officer, exposed to insults and abuses. A Russian soldier pointed his rifle at me and kept his weapon aimed at me for many minutes. He came up to me this way twice, then left shouting: "Mussoglini, Ghitler, Italianski kuligani!" (Mussolini, Hitler, Italian criminals)… *and probably sons of bitches and worse…*

The partisans arrived around 25th January, but unfortunately their arrival coincided with that of lice – peduculus corporis *– which infected me and many others with fleck typhus, with the ensuing high fever and delirium. My feet wounds, despite Volterrani's attention, got infected, expelling pus, shrapnel and pieces of leather sole. I still remember the lice migrating on the floor of our room, in single file like ants, and when they left a heap of rags it meant that the owner of that heap had died, with the lice now intent to locate another host with warm blood.*

From then on, we were put on a hyper-healthy diet, with no proteins, no fats, or carbohydrates, vitamins, etc. Now and then we had sudden and unstoppable diarrhoea. The floor of the room became covered in congealed excrement, hard as stone. If you remember, we could not shut the door because of a cone of frozen urine that no one managed to remove.

The village well contained at least one human corpse but, given the very low temperature of the water, the putrefaction must have generated only a modest amount of microbes, probably not dissimilar to today's European norms for ice-cream.

In March I started to take my first painful steps, with my foot still spewing pus. I had found a pass and together with a colleague started taking away the numerous corpses from the hospital. Luckily they were very light and we threw them into a common grave, without distinction of name or nationality. On our way back we knocked at the door of some isbe *(little houses), where with luck they would give us a potato. Other less lucky colleagues, instead of receiving food, received a bullet, as almost happened to me around*

Easter; fortunately the Russian soldier was drunk as a skunk.

I later eventually arrived at Suzdal with its spies and Soviet "converts", real or fake. My worst memory is being questioned at length one night by the Italian émigré Rizzoli, who in sending me back to my cell warned: "Buogo, you will never return to Italy!" I did not sleep for two months, waiting for the dreaded Davaj na Sibir! *(Off to Siberia!), that luckily never materialised.*

My best memory is the Russian girl with the big knockers, Valja Korova, who used to walk across our lager every morning.

I was repatriated in July 1946, without having once received news from my family, who had written to me twice a week via the Red Cross and the Vatican.

That was the end of Buogo's letter.

Towards spring I painfully started coming back to life, pestered by the good Volterrani who, swearing and cursing, wanted me to teach him English and to describe America to him. I remember him in his room, mocking Camino because of his frostbitten heel and his clothes crawling with lice. At the same time, he was extracting shrapnel from the legs of Givanni, who was lying beside me.

Boero had acquired an ugly little dog, but it vanished sometime in March. The animal had been dispatched, before being cut into small pieces and put to boil in a pan. The skin was left on top of the stove, perhaps to dry and make gloves from. Passing by, Boero spotted the skin and realised the fate of his dog. In a fit of rage, he took the meat, poured bleach over it and buried it outside in the snow, some way from the hospital. The meat was eventually found and washed repeatedly. It was still cooked into an excellent stew. Even I participated in the feast. I couldn't chew, but I could swallow, and I particularly savoured the gravy by keeping it in my mouth.

On Easter Day, the guards were absent, perhaps drunk, and some of the village women came to see us. One of them approached my camp bed and put two small boiled potatoes in my hand. How good they tasted, and the gesture struck me as very touching.

May arrived and, with the spring warmth, I was carried outside. Lying on the steps of the hospital, I managed to pick a few camomile flowers. I ate them ravenously.

That is all I remember of Podgornoje. It's a place I would gladly visit again, because it is where – with luck – I should have been buried.

TOWARDS SIBERIA

ON 23RD MAY, WE received the order to leave. I was carried to a hut where I managed to strip and my clothes were taken to be washed and fumigated. Naked, I was taken to a separate room with a few showers, but I couldn't manage to stand. The water was cold, I had no soap and the POW next to me dropped dead. He was carried outside. I kept upright by holding on to the water pipes, too weak to wash. I asked myself why he had died and not me.

The water was eventually turned off and, still naked, I was accompanied to an open window, where I was given a sheet to cover myself. Sitting on the windowsill with two other POWs, we looked like the three proverbial monkeys. Women passing by gave us a few boiled potatoes. God bless them.

When I was given back my clothes, I realised that my trousers and jacket, both lined with lamb's fur, had shrunk and were no longer usable. They gave me the clothes of a dead POW instead. With this, I hit one of my lowest points, feeling both unlucky and very depressed. Those clothes had saved me from freezing to death on the front line and, without them, I felt lost.

On 24th May we were loaded onto railway cattle wagons. I felt more ill than ever. I had managed to acquire more bandages, but my head wound was still spewing pus. They took me to one of the wagons and I managed to find a place to lie down, but we were very crowded. After an unknown length of time the train stopped and I was again loaded onto a wheel barrow. We reached what looked like stables or warehouses. I was taken to a basement and put on the earthen floor. A Russian soldier asked: *"Kak imia? Offizier? Da?"* (What's your name? Are you an officer? Yes?") I replied: *Da*. Then he asked: *"Kristiania?"* *"Da"*, I repeated, of course I am, knowing that in Russian *kristiania* means agricultural worker, not Christian. Of course I'm a Christian.

That camp was called Nikrilowka, and we remained there only for a day or two. It was only much later that I learned that my friend Capt Magnani was being held in Nikrilowka. Magnani was an imposing man, even after months of prison and starvation. When the inhuman conditions in which prisoners were kept caused outbreaks of cannibalism, he formed and led an anti-cannibalism team. This patrolled the camp, armed with an iron bar, to deter those desperate enough to kill the gravely wounded and cut out their hearts and brains.

The transfer from Podgornoje and Nikrilowka had taken less than 24 hours but had considerably worsened my condition. On my departure from Nikrilowka, I was taken to the railway in a wheelbarrow, loaded onto a rail wagon and, luckily, put down against the wall, in a corner. The large doors on both sides were bolted. More than 60 of us were crammed into our wagon, mostly sitting and packed one against the other with no straw and only a blanket each. A hole in the centre of the floor was used as a toilet. During the daytime the heat was overwhelming but, at night, it was freezing. The air coming in from the window above my head, which was covered with barbed wire, allowed me to breathe a little better than the others. The atmosphere was suffocating and the stink caused by dysentery and corpses was unbearable.

We left on May 25th on a dreadful, three-week journey to the northern town of Vietluskaja, almost as far as the Urals and Siberia. We didn't reach our destination until the 12th or 13th June. Out of 60 of us who left, 12 came out alive.

At every one of the countless stops, the soldiers escorting us opened one of the doors and at last let in a breath of air. *"Skolko kaput?"* ("how many dead?") they would ask. Then they would pick up the bodies by the arms and legs and throw them down the escarpments.

At these stops, they gave us two salted biscuits each, and a bucket of water between all of us. We were dying of thirst but I found relief, by pure chance, by licking two iron bolts on the wall. The air was condensing on them.

Outside, we could hear the drunken soldiers shouting and then the train would depart again with a series of great jolts.

A sergeant sat on my right and one night he said: "I can't take any more of this. I'm dying. If you manage to get back to Italy, remember me. Take this medallion of the Virgin and the photograph of my wife and little girl from my pocket. My address is there too. My name is… and I'll give you my tin can and spoon because you haven't got one."

"Your name is so easy to remember" I replied, "that I can't possibly forget it. But you mustn't die."

Next morning he was dead, from dysentery. I took the can, spoon, medallion and his photograph. I decided not to tell the Russians he was dead because they handed out the food on a head count. However, after two days, the smell was so bad that I was not the only one trying to get rid of him. His body was taken and thrown from the railway tracks. I remembered well the cold of the corpses in Albania and Greece, but sleeping in close proximity to such deathly chill as this was much more terrible.

I had begun to suffer considerable pain in my back when I was laid out on the wooden boards. With my fingers, I managed to locate two large sores, which were hugely swollen and causing me indescribable pain. Using the dirty rags I had with me I managed to burst them and extract an amazing amount of pus. I squeezed them for several nights. The rags I had did not last long so I used any material I could find – including some that I removed from corpses.

Not far in front of me was one man who groaned constantly. He tried everything he could to tend to his frostbitten foot. Large white maggots were crawling out of the pus. I lamented that I had only too often observed, with deep disgust, such blood and pus seeping from frozen wounds. By the time we reached Vietluskaja, I had forgotten the name of the man whose name I had said was so memorable. By then, I was dying too.

In the Urals

NONETHELESS, I FELT that I must not, and I could not die like the others. Although I did not care about dying, I felt it to be essential that I be reborn. Furthermore, I had a white chain with the medallion of the Virgin taken from the dead companion who had lain by my side in the goods wagon.

Twelve of us survived the journey to arrive in Vietluskaja, in the northern Urals, the boundary between Asia and Europe. We were taken to a large room where we were all made to wash ourselves, naked, with a few basins of water. Some of us could not resist drinking the water from the basins. "*Sabaka, nié kulturni* (uncivilized dogs), shouted the *sistra* or so-called nurses. Then they shaved our genitals.

I was later laid down on a bed with a straw mattress. Yes, truly a bed, and with a blanket as well. We were in a wooden building, a sort of Russian hospital and, although a village must also have been near by, I never saw it. I had no idea how many of us were there. I knew that we were isolated, that they had taken everything from me and that all I possessed was a white gown and a string with the medal around my neck. They washed my head wound with permanganate but paid special attention to the sores on my back. Once they healed, they left me with a large and permanent scar.

The wound on my head began to heal but intermittently seeped pus. It stayed open until January 1944 in Suzdal camp. The shrapnel splinter was only removed in Italy in January 1946.

They fed us twice a day here, a ladle of *kasha* (oatmeal) with, on rare occasions, some lard. In the morning, we received hot water and compote (cooked fruit) that was wonderful. During that time, Stalin proclaimed an Order of the Day whereby Italian soldiers were "prohibited from dying". As a result, we were given double and even triple rations of *kasha* – and our mortality rate increased astonishingly. Our bodies had been used to eating little or nothing and, with our stomachs virtually atrophied, this excess had a paradoxical effect and the number of deaths multiplied. Nonetheless, slowly I managed to move and go to the toilet on my own, with the help of two sticks.

I remained at Vietluskaja from the middle of June until August 1943 and finally met again my friend Ugo Camino, who was still limping because of a frostbitten heel.

Doctors were few and the *sistra* were incompetent – some of our POW colleagues had to teach them how to carry out injections. A woman doctor arrived from the Moscow Polyclinic, where she was a professor and head of ophthalmology. As she was examining me, I told her I had astigmatism, to which she replied: "What is astigmatism? Here in Russia it does not exist. It's a capitalistic disease." A Russian made a note of my name and date of birth and I went back to bed.

With the warm weather I started to go out for brief periods, in a nightgown and wooden clogs. One day we received an order to leave so we started out on foot. I travelled in style – on a handcart. After a few hundred metres we reached another "hospital" similar to ours, built with wood, but with watch-towers at the four corners. The building was about 20 metres away from the barbed wire, providing some space to walk about.

There were between 100 and 200 of us, but also a few Romanians and Magyars. They spoke Russian and functioned as interpreters, using German which a few of us spoke. They put us wounded officers in a room on the first floor: Givanni, Zotti, Rotelli, Camino, myself and a Lieut Belardo. This new officer did not appear to have any wounds and became the liaison between us and the camp commissar, a suspicious character and member of the NKVD[17] who was making enquiries about us. We all became careful with our words in Belardo's presence.

Later, we were joined by a "Capt" Martinelli, who did not appear to be an officer at all. We started to make fun of him and he became furious and threatened to poke my eyes out. Later identified as a private, he was a large man, in obvious good health, and used to carouse with the *sistras*, eating and drinking with them behind our backs.

My physical state started to improve. I began to negotiate the stairs with my two sticks and to go out, walking around the building first once, then twice, then five times. I started to think about escaping and mentioned this to Camino, who was enthusiastic. "It's far from impossible", he said, "we need to find where we can go over or under the fence, then continue walking south-west. The population will help us with food and clothes." I already knew some Russian and Camino was an intellectual so he would be a useful partner. We could go under or jump over the fence on a moonless night, probably from the *ubornaja* (latrine). But we needed to regain our fitness first and also to get hold of shoes and two extra blankets. For the time being we postponed the venture until the end of September.

In the meantime, we were told that the norm for our daily food rations as POWs would comprise a ladle of *kasha* (oatmeal porridge) twice a day, 300 grams of bread (barley or rye – sometimes with added hay – badly cooked and heavy, which we received during all our time as prisoners), 30 grams of fat (often substituted by wax or paraffin), 20 grams of sugar and 5 of tobacco. Three times a day we also received *ciai* (tea), really just hot, coloured water. We could have as much of that as we wanted. This was the norm and everything in Russia was based on it – food, work and any other activity. Communism itself was based on the norm of each citizen. In practice, however, we rarely received the norm. One day, *sistra* Galina, when distributing sugar on little pieces of paper, gave me much less than my allotted 20 grams. When I brought this to her attention, she took my ration, turned away and spat on it, then gave it back to me saying: "Happy? Now it weighs more." I ate it anyway, sugar and spittle.

The Russian tobacco – *makhorka* – came from the minced and dried leaves, bark and wood of a plant. It smelled of rotten fish, but after a short while we got used to it. Unless you possessed a pipe, it was smoked in cigarette paper. We made this from a two-page newspaper published fortnightly in Italian, *L'Alba*, a copy of which was given to every eight prisoners. It was a small publication full of Communist rhetoric, edited by the Italian Communist émigré Palmiro Togliatti[18], who was aided and abetted by soldiers and officers converted to Communism. Its aim was to destroy the moral fibre of prisoners and prepare them to assist in the launching of Communism once they got back to their homeland. We POWs used to divide the paper among us for cigarette paper and for "bodily use". Later, the publication became larger, and we happily continued to use it for both purposes.

In August 1943 I managed for a few days to become part of the team that peeled potatoes. They gave me a knife that I had to give back as soon as I had finished. I was delighted and eagerly ate the raw potato peels.

When I was walking round our building I found a piece of pine wood, half a brick and a short section of barbed wire. The wood was not too hard and, heating the wire on a small fire I had made near a wall, and with the help of the brick, I finally managed to drive two holes into the wood and to furnish myself with a makeshift pipe. To light the fire I used *spichki*, the primitive matches that the Russians gave us to smoke. My pipe came back from Russia and is still with me today.

Seeing that no one had bothered me during this work, I decided to make myself a knife. Next to the main entrance was a small barrel of sand, to be used in case of fire. I removed one of the two barrel hoops and broke a piece off it, then returned what was left to the barrel. I then bent the piece of iron I kept to make a handle. What became the blade was patiently filed with my brick. I made the blade red hot over a small fire and immediately immersed it in cold water and … there was my knife! I was delighted with the result and hid it by burying it near the building. Unfortunately, after a few days it disappeared. I was disheartened, but I eventually went back to the barrel, broke a second piece off the iron hoop and made another knife.

Figure 15: On the Russian front in the winter of 1942

September came, then October and Camino and I decided to delay our escape. Physically we were not yet in shape. The snow arrived. One morning in November I heard a curious noise that I thought I recognized from the days when, as a student, I had crossed Egypt on my way back to Italy. It was impossible, I thought. Surely not? And yet … yes, there it was again, the unmistakeable sound of a camel. Several of them appeared, walking in single file. I called my colleagues and over we were told later that here the Russians used them for transport. With their long fur they could handle the cold and were far more hardy than deer.

We learned other important things about the Russians and came to understand the abysmal ignorance in which we in western Europe lived. For instance, I was made aware that Verdi and Puccini were Russians and that only us poor capitalists thought they were Italian. The first steam locomotive was invented by Petrov, of course a Russian and not by Stephenson while the telegraph had been invented by Prof Popoff, way before Marconi had the idea. But now, thanks to the Soviets and Big Papa Stalin, we were cured of our ignorance, though the locals could not understand how come we were that familiar with the operas of Verdi and Puccini.

I realised I was not going to die from my wound, but two concerns remained on my mind. The first was a continuous headache, for which the Russians gave me pills. I wanted them and the other prisoners to continue to think I still suffered from vertigo, even though in reality I was much better. Unfortunately, the headaches were real. The second preoccupation was that the political commissar had summoned me, via Lieut Belardo, and had ordered me to write my autobiography. This became a regular occurrence every three or four months, or whenever we were transferred to another POW camp.

They wanted to know everything: my studies, my family, my parents' occupation. I told them that my mother was a US citizen and, despite knowing that my family was in Dresden, I told them she was in the United States. In addition, I told them that she came from a US family of well-known diplomats, that her cousin was ambassador to Greece and a colleague of Ambassador Harriman who was posted in Moscow. It was all true, except that my mother was still in Germany. I asked permission to write to Ambassador Harriman, asking him to inform his colleague MacVeagh in Greece that I was wounded, but still alive. The commissar seemed interested and sent my letter to Moscow, to ascertain if it corresponded to the truth. During my time as a POW I was asked to rewrite that letter to Ambassador Harriman, then considered a good friend of the Soviet Union, another four times!

I remember another POW, a Doctor Welzer, from Graz in Austria who became a good friend of Camino and myself. I was sorry to lose touch with him on leaving the hospital.

The camp had some excellent chess players and we started to hold tournaments. A group of German and Hungarian players used to shout their moves from their room: "C2 to D4!" We replied in the same way from our room.

A Romanian prisoner claimed to be an expert in reading the future, at the modest price of one tobacco ration. I have never been superstitious, but gave in to his insistence that he read my hand. Surrounded by a crowd of prisoners, he bent over my hand and exclaimed: "This is a very special and unusual case! The lines show that you died twice and twice came back to life!" I replied that he was correct, as I had survived first the shipwreck, then my head wound. He continued: "Now that you have been born again, you will live a long and healthy life, you will find a job, get married and you will have three children!" "Thanks", I said, "if only that could come true..." I gave him a double ration of tobacco.

On 23rd December 1943 a small group of us suddenly left Vietluskaja. Camino and some others had left a couple of days earlier. When we reached the train, we were searched and the guards found my knife. *"Davaj, sabaka, yop tvoj mat"* ("Move, dog, fuck your mother!") I was repeatedly kicked into the snow. We were locked in a special wagon for the transport of criminals and the guards were warned that I was a dangerous prisoner.

During the night we were infested by enormous bed-bugs. They did not bite me, but tickled my skin and emitted a nauseous smell. After two days we left the train at Vladimir, transferred to a horse cart and were driven to Camp NKVD 160, Suzdal. The temperature was minus-35 and we were all wounded, amputees or severely affected by frostbite. On reaching the main gate, we were directed to a large building that the Russians also used as an infirmary. My wound was examined. I had difficulty in walking and still had to use my two sticks.

"Did the shrapnel enter here?"

"Yes."

"But where did it exit from?"

"It didn't. It's still there, in my head."

"Nievozmosjen! (Impossible!)"

They didn't believe me and examined my head from every angle, but had to concede there was no exit wound. *"Bolshoj ranien!"* (very severely wounded), they exclaimed. Then, pushing me to one side: *"Davaj, sabaka!"* (move along, dog) [19]

IN A MONASTERY JAIL

BECAUSE OF MY WEAKNESS, I was put into quarantine. I emerged after two weeks, and ventured out into our new detention centre, Camp NKVD 160. I found myself among many Italian officers, most of those who had survived having been sent here.

Camp NKVD 160 was near the holy town of Suzdal, about 300km north-east of Moscow and 40km from Vladimir. It's large monastery had been famous since the 9th century, despite being destroyed once by the Tatars, then twice by the Poles, in 1238 and in 1600. It was one of the more famous religious centres of Russia.

Empress Catherine the Great (1729–1796) had a 1.2km brick wall built around it, about 12 metres high and with 12 circular or octagonal towers. The entrance tower was square and 22 metres high. In the 18th century, the monastery had 10,000 male serfs and was endowed with large tracts of land. Empress Catherine, who was renowned for her intellect and corresponded with Voltaire and Grimm, was also known for her many lovers, among them Gorloff, Potemkin and Suvoroff. She kept the last imprisoned for over 40 years, until he died, in the tower near the entrance.

Of all the concentration camps I saw, this was without doubt the most beautiful. Its churches had steeples with golden onion domes that, under the new regime, had been turned into depots, refectories and baths. In the south-eastern part of the monastery a long, two-storey building housed the monks' cells. Since 1784 these had been used to jail those condemned for crimes against religion and then, under Stalin, to jail political prisoners and POWs. Today it remains an important tourist centre, even though guides never mention that, between January and April 1944, more than 3,000 POWs died within its walls, nearly all Italians, from hunger, typhus and dysentery.

Once, when I was digging in front of the building occupied by German officers, I remember finding a skull and placing a lit cigarette between its teeth. And, when I was stealing potatoes in a room that had been converted into a depot, I amused myself by tearing plaster off the walls to expose 16th century polychrome frescos that had been covered by the Soviets. They were determined to remove any trace of religious sentiment. We were among the first who tried to bring back to light the splendour of the art that Communism was trying to annihilate. Let future tourists admiring this town remember. Sadly, they will no longer be able to admire the skull smoking its cigarette.

In the meantime, I was slowly emerging into a new life. For the whole of 1943, from 16th January until Christmas, I had struggled, maybe unconsciously, not to lose hope and die. However, by nature I loved risk and my profound taste for danger had sustained me. Nearly all those around me had died.

I could not chew, because the wound had distorted my jaw and I could not close my mouth. I slept with my left eye open, because of the paralysis affecting the left side of my face. My colleagues used to gather to see me sleep and to laugh at me. However, my teeth, which had wobbled in the first few months, slowly firmed up. I did not lose them. Perhaps my heart, lungs and physical constitution that had enabled me to compete in our Olympic team came to my rescue. However it happened, I had survived and was in a better state than I appeared.

I don't know how I had contemplated escaping and walking to Italy. Today I realise how impossible this would have been. However, the desire to gain my freedom always remained. I felt I had to give the Russians and everyone else the impression that I was more incapacitated than really was the case.

Emerging from my quarantine I again met two of my father's cousins, brothers Pio and Vittorio (Toio) Paolozzi, who had been in my boarding school in Rome between 1924 and 1928. They were both in the cavalry, Pio a sergeant and his younger brother a lieutenant. From their Polish mother they had acquired a good knowledge of Russian and Pio had become a *pirivochek* (interpreter). This gave him favoured status and kept him on good terms with the *Kommandatura*[20]. Without delay, Pio had me transferred to his cell No 6, joining Toio, two other officers and a sergeant, who was also an interpreter. Our cell was one of the smallest and we were cramped, but I was grateful for Pio's assistance, even though I remained cautious.

Then, in the middle of one night, as often happened, Pio was summoned by the NKVD at the *Kommandatura.* The following day, visibly upset, he confided to me that the Russians had asked for information on our chaplain, Don Giovanni Brevi. "Look, Toni, see if you can help me. I know nothing of this priest, whom I dislike and who probably behaved quite badly with us prisoners, as did others of his sort. You may know more about him. Can you come up with anything?" I replied that I did not know anything in particular about Don Brevi, but that he had always appeared to me to be a decent person (in fact, I had always held Don Brevi[21] in high regard and maintained a strong friendship with him). This development concerned me, but I remained friendly with Pio, who taught me a lot about what was happening in the camp.

From Pio and later many other colleagues I learned that the group of Italian officers in Suzdal was riddled with spies and informants and that an Italian émigré had been placed in our midst to coordinate them all, on the instructions of the NKVD. The Russians were trying to convert Italian POWs to Communism, to help them gain power at a later date in Italy and if necessary eliminate those who baulked at their healthy Soviet propaganda. With this objective in mind, an Anti-Fascist School had been set up near Moscow. From here, two senior Italian officers, Col Naldoni and Col Bianchi, both traitors who had sold out to the Soviets, had been sent to our camp as heads of the prisoners and to lord it over us. They were joined by several other officers, some of whom had been excellent frontline commanders, but who had converted, and now openly sided for Communism against Italy.

I felt safer with a few people whom I knew well from before arriving in Suzdal, such as my battalion commander on the Quota Cividale, Lieut-Col Zacchi, who was totally faithful to the King, Gen Ricagno, commander of the Julia division, who told me there in Suzdal that he would put my name forward for the Medaglia d'Oro to recognize my behaviour on the *Galilea,* my friends Camino, Toio Paolozzi, Bracco and Grosser, and a few others. However, it was difficult to identify all the informants and I became increasingly cautious – the danger of dying from wounds, disease or starvation had receded, but only to make way for this new and more insidious threat.

Despite this constant worry, I started to settle down. The food was the usual *kasha* – oat or millet porridge – but at times we received only dry nettles. Their taste and nutritional value was nil. The daily bread ration of 300g continued to arrive half cooked and appeared half its weight, but it had to make do.

Many of my colleagues climbed the trees to steal crows' eggs from the nests and some managed to catch the birds themselves. I could not imitate them, as I was still in a weakened physical state and in any case I could not have brought myself to eat those birds, as I had often seen them feasting on corpses in Albania, Greece and Russia. In our camp between every two cells a small fireplace gave onto the corridor and each one of us was given 1kg of wood per day to use for heating. It was there that we cooked any potatoes or meat that we managed to scrounge, despite our guards.

Close to the Italian part of the camp about 20 soldiers, mainly Italians, also lived. They carried out maintenance work and repairs and lived separately from us. On arrival, some of them had declared themselves to be officers, but they had been found out.

Each POW had a small bag made from a piece of linen and I kept my spoon in mine. To my surprise Pio was able to obtain a real pen-knife for me. Every week, we received a clean bed sheet, a shirt and a pair of long underwear in coarse fabric. I was also able to get a *katiuscia*, a lighter made from a piece of flint, a length of rope and a broken nail file. I was constantly picking up anything that might prove useful: a nail, some string or a piece of metal. With a piece of barbed wire I made two needles and managed to undo a bit of my sheet to obtain some thread. From a Romanian POW I bought a piece of aluminium for some tobacco and with my pen-knife, a nail and a lot of patience I made myself a comb, which I still keep.

At about that time, I started to enquire about who might still be alive of my Gemona battalion and decided to make a note of the names. Placing a piece of broken glass on the lamp in our cell generated lampblack which, mixed with water and soap, became ink. Then, with a crow's feather I made a quill and from the branch of an elder bush a pen, which allowed me to write on whatever scraps of paper I could find. The Soviets had forbidden us to keep records of our dead so I hid my notes in the lining of my coat. My enquiries at Suzdal established that, of 46 officers of the Gemona only two were left, Lieut Sensale, who had saved my life, and me.

Since the end of my quarantine period I had been able to move about the camp and had noticed a small separate house near the quarantine building where a German general was confined alone. In contrast to most other German high officers, he had not removed the Wehrmacht eagle from his uniform. It was Gen Artur Schmidt[22], deputy commander of the German Sixth Army led by Field Marshal Von Paulus at the battle of Stalingrad. He had been taken prisoner in February 1943. The Russians considered Gen Schmidt an obstinate opponent to their propaganda and sent him to our Camp 160. He was kept isolated from his colleagues, over whom he still exercised considerable influence.

I got to meet Gen Schmidt when, by chance, he managed to save my life. The path where POWs were allowed to walk passed in front of his hut with its little front garden. It was strictly forbidden to leave the path, shortly beyond which a barbed wire fence ran, from which a grass strip 100 metres wide stretched to the outer wall of the lager. The armed sentries manning the wall had an order to shoot anyone who left the path. One day, hobbling with my two sticks, famished as I was, I ventured on to the grass and extended my hand through the barbed wire to pick some camomile flowers to eat. A sentry pointed his gun at me, shouting *"Stoij!"* (Stop!) I had not realised the danger, but Schmidt saw what was about to happen and started shouting and gesticulating. Then he had me taken away. Luckily for me, he was an important prisoner and without his intervention I may well have been shot.

We became friends. He was born in Hamburg, his mother was British and he had been military attachè in Moscow before the war, although he was still quite young at the time. We communicated in English. I soon became his only point of contact with other German officers who had refused to remove the eagle from their uniforms. I used to visit this little group of officers and gave them English lessons, receiving tuition in German in exchange.[23]

My stay at Suzdal was cut short when, at the beginning of February 1944, I was transferred to Krasnojegorsk, a punishment and investigation camp. I had not fully understood the dangers around me. It was only later, on my return to Suzdal in April 1944 and with the help of a few good friends such as Fiocchi, Camino and Paolozzi, that I realised our environment demanded extreme caution. This needs explaining in more detail.

SOVIET POLICY

THE RUSSIANS WERE already looking at the post-war period and were organising the foundations of solid Communist parties across European nations as a base for gaining power. POW officers were excellent recruiting material, in terms of intellectual ability and discipline, for conversion to Communism.

One of the Russians' first steps was to send among us numerous Italian émigrés[24], who had left Italy because of their anti-

Fascist views, and many of whom had become more Russian than the Russians themselves. They were in the main poor, ignorant people, who saw in us their eternal enemies and they would stoop to anything to ingratiate themselves with the Soviets. They thought we Fascist invaders had no right to life. Reporting to the Political Police, their job was to identify possible informants who, in exchange for more food, better shoes or work in the canteen, would convert to Communism and spy on colleagues, reporting elements deemed hostile to Soviet propaganda. Sadly, many of these "elements" were sent away and vanished, usually condemned to death or to 20-25 years forced labour in Siberia. One of these was my friend Cpt Dante Jovino, whose death sentence was commuted to 25 years. He was repatriated in 1954, after Stalin's death.

I well remember the names of some of these émigrés who went back to Italy after the war and who bear responsibility for the deaths of hundreds of our people: D'Onofrio, Rizzoli (who was placed with us in Suzdal), Fiamminghi, Roncato, Signora Torre and others. All of them were under the authority of Palmiro Togliatti, also known as Ercole Ercoli, also known as Mario Correnti (cowardice makes people reluctant to disclose their real name).

After the war, Togliatti was helped by the US to return to Italy, where he became an MP and Minister for Foreign Affairs in the new democratic government. This assistance by the Allies was logical, as Britain and the US would never have won the war without the Soviet Union on the eastern front. During the war they supplied the USSR with materiel, food, weapons, vehicles and ammunition (the shrapnel that wounded me in the head was made in the US). After the war, the Allies continued briefly to use Communism to destroy any national sentiment in Italy and Germany, until they realised the true intentions of the Soviets.

Out of 600-650 POWs, I noted the names of 26 informants and another 28 officers who openly converted to Communism. But maybe other colleagues could add to that list…

UNDER INVESTIGATION

WHEN POWS HAD BEEN DENOUNCED by informants, or for whatever reason had came to the attention of the NKVD, they were always summoned in the middle of the night. Psychologically, this was the best time to catch people at their lowest ebb, when fear of moral and physical torture was at its highest. It was the best time to weaken and squeeze useful information out of people and the Russians were masters at this. At Suzdal, it was always a particular guard, whom we had nicknamed *Kak Familia* (what's your surname), who arrived in the dead of night with his petrol lamp. He used to bang the door open and give the nearest POW the name of the prisoner who had been chosen for interrogation, so that he could be identified and taken to the *Kommandatura.*

I was not surprised when my turn arrived and *Kak Familia* came for me one night. I found myself at the *Kommandatura*, but alone with a Russian officer and without the usual émigré assisting in the questioning and interpreting. I was asked for the same information as at Vietluskaja and to write a detailed history of my life for which I was given sheets of paper and a pencil.

Then, to the great interest of the Russian, I rewrote the letter to Ambassador Harriman in Moscow and for this I was given pen and ink. I tried my best to write exactly what I written a month earlier at Suzdal. The officer offered me a *papirosa* (Russian cigarette) and some *ciai* (tea). Later I learned that the importance of your questioner could be judged by the type of cigarette offered – luxury or standard, and by the glass in which the *ciai* was served – porcelain or tin. During the whole of this interview I was not asked for any information on my colleagues, which surprised me. The Russian only asked me: "*Vi pirivochek, da?*" (You an interpreter, yes?), knowing that I had learned some Russian at Krasnij Partisan in November-December 1942. That was all.

Why had my colleagues come out of their interviews so cowed and demoralised and why had I not received the same treatment? After returning to our cell I informed Camino and the Paolozzi brothers, who warned: "Be very careful!" In the certainty that I would be questioned again, I did my best to remember what I had written, especially the letter to Harriman.

Suddenly, one February night I received another visit from *Kak Familia* but, instead of being taken to the *Kommandatura* for questioning, I was put on an old bus and taken with a few others to Lager 27A, near Krasnojegorsk, 30km west of Moscow. It housed about 6000 POWs, mainly Germans. An underground jail and barbed wire were visible near a little lake east of the camp. Further away was Camp 27B, where the Anti-Fascist School was. Here, selected POWs attended its courses. Once the course was finished and exams passed, the candidate could gain membership of the Communist Party and Russian citizenship. Party membership was especially prized, as comparatively few USSR citizens were given this privilege.

I arrived in Krasnojegorsk with a little bag, my walking stick and a German overcoat to guard against the cold and was placed in the middle berth in a three-tier bunk bed. Thirteen of us Italians were there, most of them Communist converts or informants. Some might have been genuinely interested in Marxism-Leninism, but the others were as dangerous as snakes. I did my best to remain on good terms with them. A few officers were also firmly anti-Soviet, and in time they became good friends of mine, especially Capts Dante Jovino and Melchiorre Piazza.

Jovino was a captain in the Carabinieri (military police) and was at Lager 27 because he had been accused of killing over 300 civilians in a Russian village. The NKVD insisted that they had witnesses. Jovino had been taken several times to the Lubjanka jail in Moscow for interrogation and was in a depressed state.

One day, sitting in a corner of the camp half hidden by a shed, Jovino and I saw Romanian and Hungarian POWs using axes and knives to break open the heads of corpses and extract their gold teeth. Jovino was horrified: "Toni, we must never forget this, if we ever return."

Capt Piazza was a chemical engineer from Milan and had found himself at Lager 27A because the Russians wanted him to remain in Russia after the war and work for them. He had also been sent several times to the Lubjanka to be interrogated, as Lager 27A was also a destination where the Russians kept prisoners of particular interest to them.

Other, well-known people were held at 27A, including Ana Pauker, later a leader of the Romanian Communist Party, Maj Mueller, a German ace who shot down close to 300 enemy planes and who was himself shot down by ground fire, two German engineers involved with the V2 rocket programme, and others whose names I have forgotten.

My friendship with Jovino, Piazza and a few others did not diminish my cautiousness. A library at central *Kommandatura* had, apart from *Questions on Leninism* by Jozif V Stalin, some French books by Alexandre Dumas. I became friends with the librarian, Mrs Stern, a member of the NKVD, who spoke to me in English and was always polite and intelligent. There I also met a little German man who told me he had studied at the University of California and wanted to refresh his knowledge of Japanese, a language I had also briefly studied in Italy, at Naples. However, he seemed strange and his English was too basic for him to have studied in the US. Together, we tried to remember the characters of the Katagana and Hiragana alphabets, but without much success. Shortly afterwards, the little German vanished. I understood then that, rather than being German, he was a Russian sent to glean more information on me. It was an investigation centre after all and the Russians were trying to put together as much information on me as possible.

One day, a Jewish NKVD officer, Lieut El Perin, was beating a German POW with a stick, and I was trying to separate them. The lieutenant then turned on me, hitting me with his stick. He kicked me all the way to the camp entrance. There, he took out his pistol to shoot me. A colleague restrained him and I was taken instead to the underground jail. There I found myself on bare ground, cold and in the dark. I was fed with black bread and hot water.

An Italian, Capt Giorgio Rotolo, a surgeon, was also there. I can't remember why he was an honourable companion. We got talking and, when I mentioned my wound, he said: "That's no problem. Come to me. After an X-ray, I will put you to sleep and operate on you. I will extract the shrapnel and you'll wake up cured. And if you don't wake up, you won't care, will you? Come to see me, I'll be expecting you." Dear Rotolo, he was serious and spoke as if it were unimportant. I agreed, saying that, whatever about being a respected surgeon for me, as he was in Milan, the difference between life and death was indeed minor, death being a triviality to be laughed at. He concurred: "You are absolutely correct," and offered me a cigarette.

By the weak light of his match I glimpsed an inscription on the wall. Someone may have carved it with a nail. *"Exoriare aliquis nostris ex ossibus ultor,"* it read. The line, by Virgil, had probably been scrawled by a German POW. "Arise from my bones, o avenger, whoever you may be". "By God," I said to myself, "how true."[25]

I was summoned by the NKVD for further questioning only 24 hours after being freed. The person who interviewed me was a civilian, but from the way the guard saluted him and gave him the porcelain *stakan* (glass) with the *ciai,* I took him to be an important official. He was extremely polite and, speaking in Russian mingled with a little French, enquired about my health. He added that it had been a mistake to put me in jail and that I should have been referred to the Moscow Polyclinic. Also, he said I could contact Mrs Stern whenever I thought necessary. He enquired about my past and offered me large perfumed cigarettes. I told him that, in my true opinion, Russian was a beautiful language, that I would welcome the possibility to learn it better and that I never had anything against the Russian people.

JOE SCHMIDT

AT THE NEW CAMP I met several other POWs, mainly Germans but also a few Dutch and Belgians. They had all fought with the Germans. I got on best with Joseph Schmidt, a *Feldwebel* (sergeant-major) of the Logistics Corps. His family had emigrated from Germany to Canada when he was a child. He was a naturalised Canadian and worked as a fur trapper in summer and, in winter, fished on the Great Lakes. He went to work in China, then Japan shortly before that country joined the Axis. At the beginning of the war he was sent back to Germany, where the Wehrmacht recruited him as a logistics specialist. We communicated in English, his mother tongue, and we used to sing popular songs together:

Oh get me a home, where the buffalo roam,
Where the deer and the antelope play,
Where seldom is heard, a discouraging word,
And the skies aren't cloudy all day...

I felt I could trust Schmidt. He told me that three American POWs were being held in our camp. Allied military kept in detention? It seemed impossible but, with the Russians, one never knew. This was, after all, an NKVD investigation camp.

One day, Joe confided in me that he was thinking of escaping. I was immediately interested in his plan and told him so. We had both thought about organising an escape in the past and we could now join our efforts.

To get back in shape, Joe went to Krasnojegorsk village three times a week with a work party and, because it was still cold, he had to wear padded overalls. All I needed to do was to get another set of overalls and, unobtrusively, join the work party. Once we arrived at the factory, we could then discreetly make our escape, heading south.

Joe wanted to travel at night, hide during the day and follow the rivers. I agreed and was sure his trapping experience in Canada would make us successful. For my part, I gave a guard some bread and tobacco and was given a geography book belonging to his daughter, who had just finished school, in exchange. As I was still studying Stalin's book on Leninism, I obtained from Mrs Stern two note blocks and some additional paper. Using these and a pencil from a German POW, I made two identical maps of the itinerary Joe and I had researched and planned in some detail. I had also made a rudimentary compass, using a needle I found at the camp and magnetised by holding it against the magnet of one of Suzdal's many loudspeakers. When placed on something small that floated, such as a small leaf or even a hair, it unerringly indicated north. It was a useful object and, even if found during a search, it was outwardly innocent.

We planned to leave at the end of March, and head south from Krasnojegorsk towards the Moscova River near Gorki, where it joins the Volga. We would then follow the Volga for about 1,000km, until we reached the point where the Don was about 50km away, just before Stalingrad. From there we would head in the direction of Rostoff and enter the Caucasus. We had been informed that Soviet authorities in Georgia and Armenia were trying to stop people emigrating south, so we had decided to head towards Armadir, then Tuapset on the Black Sea. Following the coast, we would reach Poti and, bypassing the border port of Batumi, enter Turkey and direct ourselves towards the sources of the Euphrates. From there we could either go towards Aleppo and the Mediterranean, or follow the Euphrates until we reached the Persian Gulf. This last option was our preferred route.

This plan may now appear impossible, but we were desperate to escape and, for us, time was no object. We were also aware of and had planned how to deal with the enormous difficulties along the way. All escape attempts from Camp 27 had failed, with escapees being recaptured within 24 hours for two main reasons. Either the guards had used Alsatian dogs to track them or they had been betrayed by children. Ukrainians and Cossacks were usually ready to give food and help to escaped POWs but their children had all been conditioned by Soviet propaganda immediately to alert the authorities to any strangers passing through their area – even if being sheltered by their parents. Yet we were convinced that, with patience, all problems could be solved. We had planned for everything, including how to give the slip to the guard dogs. Our winter clothing would be enough for any weather and we set ourselves no time limits.

Luck was against us. A week before our escape attempt in April, when I was already feeling the tension, I was told I had to leave for Moscow, to be examined at the polyclinic for my wound. My Italian colleagues gave me 10 roubles each to buy whatever I could find for them, but I was taken to the train before being able to warn Joe.

TO THE LUBJANKA

ON THE TRAIN, I seated myself among the other passengers and no-one paid any attention to me. After half an hour we arrived at *Gorkaja Staniza* (Gorki station). I went to the toilet there, a wooden shed with ten holes in the ground in two rows. Men and women squatted together.

At the polyclinic I was told I would be X-rayed with new Agfa Zeiss equipment, just arrived from Oriental Prussia. I was told to strip to my belt. After the X-rays had been taken, we went to a large market near the station. I wanted to buy some pork meat, *svignaja tuscionka*, but bartering in kind was the only means of exchange; had I anything to offer? I had 60 roubles in all and, in the end, desperate not to come back empty-handed, I satisfied myself with a small box of 12 fruit sweets for 50 roubles. At least my colleagues could divide a treat from Moscow among themselves, something from the great Soviet people, something that in Italy would have cost less than a packet of cigarettes.

On boarding the train to go back, I noted an airfield with wooden planes, maybe designed to confuse enemy reconnaissance flights.

The X-rays taken at the polyclinic showed, to the astonishment of the Russian doctors, a large piece of shrapnel in the middle of my brain. On my return to Camp 27, Capt Rotolo was shown the X-rays and put my mind at rest. The metal in my brain was none other than a golden crown on a molar. The Russian doctors had simply misread the tangent of the radiography. I could not care less though. I was alive and that was enough for me. I immediately contacted Joe Schmidt again, who was afraid that I had vanished for good.

Soon afterwards, however, the head of our hut, Hauptman Kaufmann, an SS officer who had converted to Communism, told me to leave, this time with an escort, for the central NKVD in Moscow. I left on a small truck in the evening which automatically led me to expect the worst. I was seated in the back with a guard and, in front, another guard sat alongside the driver. When the truck finally stopped, I heard a large gate or door being opened. On stepping down, I realised I was in the courtyard of the Lubjanka, the huge state prison. It had often been described to me at Lager 27 as hell for prisoners.

With no exchange of words, my escort handed a sheet of paper to the guards and I was firmly but gently taken in their charge and searched. My walking stick was taken away. I was made to descend to the floor below via an iron, spiral staircase. A guard received me and, with another behind, they led me down a long, narrow and dimly lit corridor where, every 10-12 metres, niches receded into the walls. The floor was covered with felt. I was delivered to a cell, barely one metre by two, and three metres high, with an iron door and a peephole. The walls and the floor were of concrete. The cell was painted brown up to the height of a normal person and was stark white above. On the ceiling were four holes – for air, I imagined – and a strong light.

A number of colleagues had already been at the Lubjanka and had returned marked by their experience. They described cells where, under strong lighting, water was progressively pumped into them until it reached their throats, or narrower cells where it was forbidden to lie down and sleep. Prisoners were subjected to refined tortures to elicit confessions of actions that, more often than not, had never been committed.

It was an inhuman, surreal place. Every public clock showed a different time. The niches were cut into the corridors so prisoners would not meet. A prisoner, when about to pass another, was pushed, face inwards, into one of the alcoves. Escorts all had large bunches of keys that they jangled to alert colleagues of their presence. Speaking was absolutely prohibited in this "public place", and all guards wore felt *valenki* so they could move without being detected if they so wished.

My cell had nothing more than a bucket with a metal lid. I had no means of knowing if it was day or night.

On my arrival, with, rather than fear, a sense of fatalism, indeed curiosity, and a readiness to be patient, I sat down on my coat. Why was I here, since I had not been threatened during my interrogations? After maybe no more than half an hour, a guard with a large moustache arrived. "*Davaj!* Let's go!" he commanded and took me out into the dark corridor. He was alone so I reckoned I was not considered dangerous.

We went a long way down the corridor and finally arrived at a steel cage-lift that took us upwards. I entered a room where I found a man in civilian clothing, sitting behind a table on which were a telephone, a panel with buttons on it and a strong light that faced in my direction. The windows had no bars.

He indicated that I should sit on the chair before him. In excellent Italian, after asking for my details, he told me that the Soviet authorities had examined the case of Prisoner of War Ferrante di Ruffano, born in Florence, and had brought him to the General POW Directory to clear up some questions. I was not to be afraid because, immediately after the interrogation, I would be returned to the same lager, he said.

A guard arrived, possibly summoned via a button on the panel, with a tray bearing two white china cups filled with boiling and sweet tea. The officer took a large packet of perfumed cigarettes from a table drawer, the longest I had ever seen, and offered me one. "*Pajalusta* – you're welcome", he said with a half smile. I was amazed and nervous... what was this all about? The respect paid to this Russian by the guard suggested that he was a high-ranking official.

My life history was reeled off again, this time with precise questions being asked. He told me he had lived in Italy and had studied the language as he greatly loved the country and its people. I, having lived at length in other countries, could not possibly have such a limited outlook as that possessed by the Fascists, he suggested. The war was coming to an end and there would be little left of Italy, thanks to the Capitalist democracies of America and England. What did I expect to do?

"I have no idea as yet," I replied. "All my pre-university studying was done with the Jesuits." "Ah," he exclaimed, "They are the diplomats of the Church, which is the greatest enemy of our Soviet democracy. But rest assured that Moscow has already penetrated the Vatican and, in the near future, the Church will be neutralised from within. The whole world will change politically."

I replied that I was certain this was the case, that I had studied to enter the diplomatic service and that I regretted not knowing Russian because I loved the Russian people. I was not, I hastened to assure him, a *pirivochek*[26], but I liked the language of which, as a soldier, I had managed to learn a little while in the country. Nonetheless, Russia had a great future, I said, because it was richer and vaster than any other country.

Before dismissing me, the officer ordered me not to say anything to my fellow prisoners about this meeting. "*Dosvidanya*", he said, meaning "we'll meet again" rather than "goodbye". Apparently I was to be summoned some time in the future. He suggested that, in the meantime, I think about what I might do after my imprisonment.

The guard took charge of me again and I was escorted back to the same truck in the Lubjanka courtyard. The clock stood at nine o'clock – although it was more probably three or four in the morning. I arrived at camp as dawn broke, but in Lager 27C rather than Lager 27A nearby, possibly to avoid any contact with my former colleagues. This new camp was much larger, as it received all prisoners captured on the front who were to be distributed to camps all across the USSR. It turned out that it did not focus on investigation and punishment and seemed less dangerous than 27A, but I remained on my guard more than ever.

DEATH OF A FRIEND

THE FEW HOURS SPENT at the Lubjanka played heavily on my mind. Jovino, Piazza and the others had all spoken of it with terror. Why had I been subjected to such different treatment? The NKVD must have a good reason and the more I thought about it the more I felt a sword of Damocles over my head. I was too afraid to share my worries with anyone.

At Camp 27C I was supposed to carry out physical work and was pleased about this. However, still being considered disabled, I was assigned to making nails. I was provided with a coiled length of wire and a tool that straightened it and cut it every three or four centimetres. I had to hammer one end to make a nail head.

One day, someone pointed out the head of the Anti-Fascist School at Camp 27B to me, who was visiting our camp. Capt Diego Cadeddu was an Italian officer who had been at my high school, the Jesuit Mondragone College. He had been a star pupil, a good footballer and religious. He had finished school a few years before me and been assigned to the Corazzieri (the royal guard) in Rome, because his father was a general well known to the Royal Family. He had converted to Communism, against all the ideals and principles of his upbringing.[27] It really was him, but I kept well away. He did not recognise me.

Recent events had forced me to lay to one side my escape plan, devised in such detail and such keen hope with Joe Schmidt. The worries following my Lubjanka interrogation had also overshadowed the sadness of having to leave him. Then I received devastating news. Undaunted by my sudden departure for Moscow, he had decided to attempt the escape from Camp 27A on his own and failed almost immediately. He was recaptured in less than an hour by the dogs and was placed in solitary confinement for several days. Joe lost his mind and, just a few days after being released, had been caught again trying to dig a tunnel under the barbed wire. He was judged to be a serial offender and was sent to the underground jail. There, guards placed red-hot coals in each of his hands and forced the fists shut. Crippled, after a few days he hanged himself.

The sadness and horror I felt could not, however, bring me to give up the idea of escape. At Camp 27C I made another friend, a German pilot who had been recently captured and was awaiting transfer to another lager. He was enthusiastic about escaping and I had explained to him that, years ago, I had learned to fly in Australia, although I knew nothing of military aircraft. Provided we could avoid the dogs or being denounced by children we would locate an airfield. He was familiar with the area near Leningrad and Lake Ladoga, from where we should be able to get back to our lines… *audaces fortuna iuvat* (who dares wins).

Once again, fate decided against an escape attempt. Suddenly, my new German friend was transferred. I now felt very alone. I did not feel I could trust anyone else, especially Italian POWs, to take part in my attempts.

A few days later I was given my transfer order. The Italian soldiers were sent to other destinations, while two officers and myself returned to Camp 160, at Suzdal. There I rejoined all my colleagues.

7: THE LUBJANKA

ITALY CHANGES SIDES

B ACK IN SUZDAL, conditions had not improved. In comparison with 27A and 27C, we still did not have enough food and it was of poor quality. They often had no oats or millet to make the *kasha* and, when this happened, we were given dried nettle soup instead. Our sugar ration was not always distributed and, instead of the daily 30 grams of fat, we sometimes received wax or paraffin. The new camp commandant, Col Krastin, had placed Col Bianchi, one of our "converted" senior officers, in charge of the Italians. During the evening assembly, which we all had to attend, he used to wear the uniform of a Romanian soldier and state that a Romanian private was worth ten Italian generals.

However, to my surprise I was no longer called in for questioning by the *Kommandatura* every three to four months, as had been happening, and was never harassed by the Italian émigrés. Even so, the way Joe had ended his life and the fact that I could trust no one enough to attempt an escape with me lowered my morale. I cautiously renewed my contacts with the German officers, once again exchanging English for German lessons. We also had a *Meister Kapelle* (music master), Hauptman Adams, who composed a beautiful song for German prisoners. We often all sang it together, and he wrote down the music and words for me:

> *So weit in den land hinter Moskau,*
> > Far off in the land beyond Moscow
> *Wohl hinter dem Stachelzaum,*
> > Behind the barbed wire barrier
> *Da Sieht man gefangene Soldaten,*
> > You can see soldiers kept prisoner
> *Voll Wehmut in die Farne Schaum,*
> > Gazing afar off, full of sadness

Und wenn die kalte Sterne steigen,,
And when the cold stars appear
Und die Dammerung immer tiefer singt
And dusk inexorably falls
Kann einer nicht mehr langer schweigen
You can no longer stay quiet
Dann summt er ganz leise und singt:
and start humming a soft song:

Ich bin ein arme Plennj
I'm but a poor Plennj
Gefangen schon manches Jahr,
A prisoner for many years
Doch nach der Heimat sehnt sich.
Dreaming about my homeland
Mein Herz wohl immer dar!
Where my heart always belongs!

Wann kommt der Tag der Freiheit,
When will the day of freedom come
Wann kommt der grosse Gluck
When will I have great joy
Wann kehr ich in die Heimat,
When will I be able to come home
Die teure Wohl zuruck?
To my most precious treasure?
O schones Vaterland!
My beautiful Fatherland![28]

We were informed that, since the autumn of 1943, Italy had been declared a "co-belligerent" with the Allies. Because of this, the Soviets were now trying to form an expeditionary corps to fight against the Germans, pushing POWs to write petititions to this effect. This contingent was not created, but the efforts to do so increased the resentment between the anti-Fascist informers and those of us who remained faithful to the officer's oath. We felt isolated, in a country where propaganda had to be used all the time to keep the population cowed. We had difficulty in believing anything we were told. It was only from POWs recently "liberated" from the advance into eastern German territory that we were able to confirm the truth in the news of the steady defeat of the Germans and the debacle of the Italians.

My instinctive reaction was to ask why we should turn against the Germans whom we had fought with until now? Even assuming that Italy had been bombed into submission and the south had been invaded by the Allies, how could it be possible that so many Italians had joined the Anglo-Americans, betraying the Axis and, more importantly, betraying our national army? It was still deployed and fighting with the Germans! How could this be possible? We Italians were not born traitors. It must have been all propaganda... otherwise the rest of the world would neither forget nor forgive us.

My own thoughts were clear and precise: instead of fighting the Germans, I would have gone to Italy and put all those who had switched sides to the Anglo-Americans against a wall and shot. In which circle of the Inferno did Dante place those who betray their country? Such people cannot sink any lower.

As a result of this increased tension, those prisoners who had been identified as too "Italian", as Fascists or firm anti-Communists were sent eastwards, often to Siberia: Magnani, Don Brevi, Joli, Russo, Pennisi and others.

Among them was Lieut Italo Stagno. During one of the meetings held by the émigré Rizzoli and other officers recently arrived from the Anti-Fascist School, he had to listen to exhortations to join the Communists in Italy and to words of derision against our fallen comrades. He stood up behind me and said clearly that our duty was to bring back to Italy the flag and the faith, both intact, which thousands of our fallen brothers had bequeathed to us. Then, addressing the émigré directly, he added: "Gentlemen, we here are the deputies of our dead."[29] Soon after this episode, Italo Stagno was summoned to the *kommandatura* and I never saw him again.

I remained at Suzdal from May 1944 to April 1945, still uncertain about my future. A few Spanish officers, who had volunteered to fight against Stalin and Communism[30], were also there. I avoided them, even though I was full of admiration for them and said nothing about my participation in the Spanish Civil War on Franco's side.

The Italian officers were not compelled to work, unlike the Germans, but I was determined to regain some of my strength and wanted to imitate Camino, who had volunteered to go out with a group to chop wood a few kilometres away. However, I continued to be classed as disabled. Nevertheless, together with Lieut Bracco, a courageous officer and excellent combatant, one evening I managed to climb over the barbed wire behind the Hungarian section and reach a cultivated area. Because of the twilight we remained unnoticed there by the guards, dug up some cucumbers and returned without trouble.

On another occasion, Bracco and I walked casually to the bell tower of a disused church in the middle of the camp. A number of bricks had come loose near the bottom and Bracco was able to enter the tower and climb up the inside to the top. I could not follow him, as the vertigo I still occasionally suffered was more pronounced in the dark, so I stayed as a lookout.

At the top was a room where the Soviets kept old woollen clothes. The people had lost the right to buy clothes, so the government periodically distributed new clothing and took away the old. When Bracco returned, he had several old woollen items, from which I chose some socks. I took them apart and knitted myself a pair of heavier socks. I had already made myself three knitting needles from barbed wire and had learned from a colleague how to knit socks, including the rounded part on the heel. But, damn it, almost as soon as they were finished they were stolen. I had to start all over again with thinner wool and so had to make thinner needles. I never finished the second pair.

One day I obtained permission – at last – from the doctor who periodically examined me and gave me headache pills, to join the Beetroot Brigade. Even though still disabled, I told him I could still work sitting down. So I went with the work party. We dug the beetroots out with pitchforks and put them into bags. I ate a lot of of them, after scraping the earth away. The second day I got a shock when I thought I was urinating blood. I soon realised it was only all the beetroot I had eaten and I stopped taking part in the harvest.

When winter arrived, we amused ourselves by holding conferences at our club which also hosted theatrical presentations organised by our Gruppo Artisti. I still remember Lieut Paiella, dressed exotically as a vamp (with lovely tits), and a singer who was called Todi. We who were always famished listened to a presentation on the manufacturing of Gorgonzola cheese by 2nd Lieut Chini. And I myself even gave a conference entitled: "A world tour via Naples-USA-Hawaii-Sydney-Naples". It was quite a success.

KEEPING A RECORD

IN CAMPS 27A AND 27B the authorities encouraged POWs to absorb as much as possible on Communism, from their study and from conferences, before being sent back to Italy. Dear Mrs Stern had no difficulty in providing me with two notebooks and a pencil, of which I immediately noticed the brand: *"Karandash Sacco y Vanzetti"*. The Russian factory manufacturing pencils had been dedicated to Sacco and Vanzetti, the anarchist anti-Fascists who had had to leave Italy in 1922, only to be executed in the United States, after a trial, centring on their beliefs, that left many doubts. At the time, my father had been the Italian consul in Boston and attended the whole trial. Once, he took me with him to Sing Sing jail, where we visited the defendants. In Russia they became heroes and symbols of the proletariat.

POWs were prohibited from keeping any written material, except for notes taken at the Anti-Fascist School or at Camp 27A, or if they were about the Communist democracy and might encourage others in Europe to join the cause. The Soviet authorities were especially suspicious of memoirs or lists of the dead. When such records were found in periodic searches they were always forwarded to the NKVD.

With the paper that I was given by Mrs Stern, together with some *machorka* tobacco wrappers, and using my crow's feather nib stuck in an alderwood pen, I wrote Russian-French-German dictionaries. I then found, I forget how, some real ink and started writing down pieces of literature or poems that struck me, from Montesquieu, Zola and Hugo to Longfellow and Sholokov. These were precious to me and I took them down in minute handwriting, mixing them up with Russian grammar and lessons on Communism, Lenin and Stalin. Should my notes be discovered, these Communist notes might provide me with enough of an excuse to keep them all.

In 1945, still using *machorka* wrappers, I made my own little book from the bark of birch trees, binding it with string and wire. To these I added Russian songs, a copy of my letter to Ambassador Harriman and then – despite being severely prohibited by camp authorities – a list of officers of the Julia division, by order of unit, who had been at Camp 160. This list included the dead, the wounded and the missing in action, who we thought had been repatriated, where to and how. All this was the result of persistent but discrete enquiries with my colleagues. I had started as soon as I was well enough to write and continued compiling information at Camp 160.

The problem was how I might keep all this and bring it back to Italy. I knew I was playing with fire by keeping these records. Don Brevi, the chaplain and a friend of mine, had started such a list but was found out and ended up in Siberia. As a result, I told no-one about the notes.

I had realised, though, that, even after being sent to other camps or to Moscow, officer POWs were always returned to Camp 160 Suzdal. So, knowing I would probably be summoned back to the Lubjanka, and to take these records with me would have been suicidal, I decided to bury them in the infirmary of Camp 160. I visited it regularly for headache pills and to encourage the impression that I was still severely wounded and ill.

Government-controlled Soviet radio broadcasted the many victories of the Red Army every day as well as a steady diet of Russian national songs. It announced that American prisoners-of-war had been suffering from hunger under the Japanese and were being given only a fistful of rice a day. And they expected us to feel sympathy! We looked at one another, amazed. The Americans were like children, whining against the barbarity of their captors. A fistful of rice! If they only knew how their beloved USSR ally treated its own POWs. We would often have welcomed half that amount. On the other hand, the American soldier was used to fighting with all the comforts such as showers on the front line and seven men in logistics for every combatant. Now they were suffering, the poor dears.

Gradual improvements came in the autumn and winter of 1944-45. Lice had been eliminated for some time and we showered periodically. Soap became the size of postage stamps and we were able to use it to wash ourselves in the running water in the courtyard sinks. Even in winter, with the temperature well below freezing I washed bare-chested, drying myself with a length of sheet. Diarrhoea was still with us. It was funny to see a colonel walking about with two majors and suddenly squatting, defecating and all three then continuing their walk – "Well, as we were saying…" We were left with the hunger, and what hunger!

We struggled to make life as normal as possible. To obtain tobacco pouches or handkerchiefs we tore pieces off our sheets and, as a result, the clean sheets given out became progressively shorter. For the Russians, the use of handkerchiefs was unheard of, they were dirty, *nie kulturnii* (uncivilized). It was much more civilised to place a finger on the obstructed nostril and expel its contents to the ground.

The ingenuity of prisoners reached new heights: Lieut Viel made a pendulum clock with its mechanism entirely in wood. Gen Battisti did the same and managed to bring it back with him in 1946. POWs working with horses cut off their tails and sold the hairs for bread or tobacco to those who were able to make brushes. Socks were also made with stolen wool, taken from the same bell tower that Bracco had climbed. The Hungarians were specialists in teaching us how to knit them.

I attempted to imitate Viel by trying to carve a small medal from a piece of bone, but failed. Lieut Zuppa had become our barber and also shaved Russian officers, who gladly provided him with the necessary tools. As being shaved cost tobacco, one day I managed to open his little room, which he always kept locked, and took a razor. Since then, I had always shaved myself and could do so even without a mirror or in the dark, without soap or water. I never cut myself.

Officers received a monthly allowance of 10 roubles, whereas generals received 50, perhaps to meet some international requirement on the treatment of POWs. However, it was forbidden to spend them and in any case this would not have been possible. Spend them how and where? The population did not spend anything and received what was necessary from the state. Also, prisoners were forbidden to own more than 50 roubles, so that the money they had given and that we had saved was confiscated during the regular searches we were subjected to… such was the Soviet mentality.

The searches were meticulous. We had to wait outside our quarters and the guards looked everywhere, even under the floorboards. Then, as we re-entered, we were frisked and searched individually. We each had our own hiding places, but even when we thought we had beaten the system, we had to be careful about informers.

RETURN TO MOSCOW

ON 29th APRIL 1945, I was summoned by the *Kommandatura* and directed to an old car with two other prisoners, a Russian and a Romanian. We headed for Moscow. We arrived at the Lubjanka at night. I couldn't see anything but I heard the large front gate creaking open and knew where I was. I had taken with me some tobacco and a piece of newspaper.

My two companions vanished and the only word spoken to me was *"Davaj!"* Again, my belt and walking stick were taken from me and, with one guard leading and another following, we went down the spiral staircase. The darkness and silence were almost total, except for the guard in front jangling his keys.

We reached a small cell, much the same as the one I had been briefly kept in last time. I sat on the floor. What did they want this time? Would I be accused of being dangerously anti-Russian? I had always been careful with people who could have denounced me, if possible avoiding them altogether. Everyone knew that I was wounded in the head and disabled. I had informed no one now in Suzdal of my escape plans. I still kept in my *sciapka*, the magnetised needle I had made when plotting with Joe, but that looked innocent enough. I was also thinking about my colleagues Palmieri and Nannini, who had been condemned to be shot here in the courtyard of the Lubjanka. The executions were faked and blanks were fired, but the psychological effects were severe. Palmieri lost his mind. I should expect anything, but God knows why I was not more discouraged. I felt stronger than my physical appearance suggested. I waited... I was neither cold nor hot, neither hungry nor thirsty. What time could it have been?

Suddenly the door opened. It wasn't the man with the large moustache but a shaven Mongol. *"Davaj!"* I followed him. Walking in the dark I sometimes lost my balance and had to put my hands on the wall, but without comment from my escort. I finally reached a large office where the usual strong lamp was pointed at me. An elderly civilian at the desk said *"Pajalusta"*, politely inviting me to sit in front of him, a red file between us. I was disappointed not to see the official with whom I had spoken on my first visit.

A few moments later the door opened and another civilian came in. It was the man who had interrogated me last time. By the deferential attitude of his colleague, I understood he must be higher ranking. They both faced me and the older man said: "*Ranien, da?*" Yes, I was wounded. The conversation continued in Italian. Had I given thought to our previous conversation? Yes, I had, but even if I had the luck to be repatriated, I would not know what to do. My family was in Germany, if it still existed, and my mother and sister were probably in America.

The conversation changed tack: they had made enquiries about me and I was not like my colleagues. Yes, Russia was harsh against its enemies, but I was not a Fascist like my friends, I had an open mentality, more democratic and the only real democracy was in Russia, not in any Capitalist nation. It had been noted that several times I had stated my love for the Russian people. They continued: "Now we need people abroad who understand us. Once this war is concluded, the world will totally change." I had also thought several times about this and agreed with him.

The elder man continued: "If you agree, Great Russia can help you far more than what is now Italy, maybe even more than America. A supra-national entity, the United Nations is being constituted and will be based in the United States. Every nation will participate in it. You would be qualified to work there and we can assure you that you would obtain a very good post as an Italian, because of your studies, knowledge and family. If you accepted, what would you do?"

A button on the console was pressed and a tray was brought in with three *strakan* of good-quality porcelain and a plate of grey caviar. I was genuinely surprised, amazed. This was not what I was expecting. My surprise must have been evident. The younger man said, with a smile: "Do believe us. We are the highest authority and I can assure you that this is an exceptional step by our government. We need, however, to know how you would act in this eventuality."

My answer was simple: obviously I would remain a friend of the USSR but, to better assist them, I could not openly be seen to be a Communist. The two NKVD officials fully agreed! It was understood that, when I joined the UN, I only had to follow the directives I would receive from Moscow. During the remainder of my imprisonment I should continue to act as I had done up to now and must not show any pro-Communist tendencies.

The two friends seemed satisfied and the subject changed to... the uses of caviar, and the types and the vitamins it contained.

After a strong handshake, the guard was summoned with the pressing of another button and I was taken to the entrance of the Lubjanka. My walking stick and belt were returned to me. I boarded a small truck. Dawn was about to break. I was not tired and felt I was dreaming. Yet I could not mention what had just happened to anyone.

THE GENERALS' VILLA

TO MY SURPRISE, the truck did not take me back to Suzdal, but to an isolated, two-storey *dacha* in a large, former nobleman's estate. It was 1st May 1945, the day after Hitler's suicide. The place was known as The Villa and was used for detaining high-ranking prisoners. It was surrounded by barbed wire and dogs. I have not been able to ascertain its precise location.

The Villa housed 44 German generals, captured at Stalingrad and later on during the war. In a small, separate building were four junior Italian officers, a colonel in the Hungarian army who had fought with us on the Don, and an older Romanian general whom I liked. He was depressed, however, and shortly afterwards hanged himself.

The four Italian officers had attended the Anti-Fascist School in Lager 27B at Krasnojegorsk. I recognised their names because they had published articles in the prisoners' newspaper *Alba*, denigrating Italy. One of them, Lieut Ferio Strabucchi, from Genoa, was an Alpino with the Cuneense division who had become a fervent Communist.

I was placed with the four Italians in a small building near the villa and, although I felt ashamed to be living with them, I believed the best policy would be to befriend Strabucchi. Otherwise, he could have proved dangerous. At the same time, I studiously avoided discussing politics with him. During this first period at the villa, I was tormented day and night by the memory of my last visit to the Lubjanka. I had plenty of time to think about its significance.

The German generals were housed in the large *dacha* and, like us, all had rooms with beds, blankets and sheets. We all went to a central mess to study and read. Almost all the books were about politics, but a few others, always in great demand, were in

French or German. We were served by German soldiers and we always ate corn or millet *kasha* – but on china plates.

Col Csimatis, the terror of the camp, reigned over us all. He was a former assistant to Goebbels but had become a fervent Communist. Here he acted as commissar. We were issued with a notebook and pencil and I took notes during economics lessons, put on by Col Csimatis as part of his educational programme for the German generals.

These generals were a strange bunch. Most had removed the Wehrmacht eagle from their uniforms and, divested of their haughtiness, stopped posing as military supermen. In fact, they behaved more like lost children. At table, they cut up their bread into little pieces, spread a bit of *kasha* on it and put it aside to take to their rooms in a napkin. They played chess and draughts. On a *Machorka* cigarette wrapper, which I have kept, I wrote the names of some of these generals who had achieved fame in the war: Lieut-Gen Hell; Gen Bosch, with his moustache; Gen Brandt; Gen Troger; Gen Fredeck, an Austrian; Gen Von Dewitz, known as the "Torpedo" due to his shape; Gen Bayer; Gen Stingl, a chess champion; Gen Bome; Gen Mueller, commander of the German troops at Cassino and here called Rigoletto; and Gen Postel, who had been wounded seven times.

They fought among themselves like children over a piece of bread ("his is bigger than mine!"), or a minor possession ("that's my chair not yours"). All were servile and allowed themselves to be terrorised by Csimatis. He treated them like a herd of sheep. This reinforced my impression that the Germans are unbeatable with a leader but, without one, they are lost.

The 9th May 1945 was a special day. All through the night before the loudspeakers had blasted out more military music than usual. In the morning, the order arrived that all camp prisoners should gather to celebrate the end of the war and the defeat of Germany. We all had to toast the victory of Stalin's Great People. Affecting a strong headache due to my wound, I did not go, despite being encouraged by my companions to attend.

I left the hut and began to walk round the garden, assisted by my stick, going round the *dacha* anti-clockwise. I saw Gen Hell coming towards me from the opposite direction. He was alone. I stopped in front of him, saying: "You are the only one here. Why aren't you with the others, Sir?" He looked me in the eyes and put his hand affectionately on my shoulder, "You too, my friend," he replied. "We are the only ones not celebrating our defeat." Something cracked inside me, and I broke down in tears. It was the first and last time I cried. He was one of the highest-ranking generals and had kept the eagle on his jacket. Wordless, we continued our solitary rounds.

Two days before leaving the villa I was called for questioning, as were all POWs before a transfer. The NKVD officer was a good-looking girl who had a file with all my data. She spoke Russian to me, but I replied that I didn't know the language. She insisted that my file stated that I did. She started to go over my past and asked me if I had given myself up voluntarily to the Russians. My answer was that I had been wounded in combat and, if given a choice, I would never have allowed myself to be captured. "But how many Russians did you kill?" she asked. I replied that I commanded 81mm mortar units and that maybe the number of dead enemies was too great to count. I was furious, perhaps because of being questioned by this young woman but also because the conversation in the Lubjanka may have given me courage. The conversation ended.

Outside, I was later behind the *dacha* where cauliflowers were cultivated. I wanted to eat some raw vegetables but was undecided whether to take one. A group of guards arrived and picked one. To our surprise they cut all the large parts off and kept only the stalk, which they began eating. *"Pacemù?"* (Why?), I asked. They replied that the head was for pigs and POWs. "But we know that you like cauliflower soup," I ventured, "although you cook it with sour green tomatoes." "Yes," they replied, "it is delicious, and not with ripe tomatoes. They are insipid and full of water."

On 16th May, all the Italians left and were taken back to Suzdal.

PLOTTING A STRATEGY

MY TWO VISITS TO THE LUBJANKA proved to be of great significance. Both times, I was not brought back after the visit to the camp where I had been staying, to avoid my colleagues knowing what had happened. As it happened, I never divulged what I had been told during the interviews, neither to other NKVD officials questioning me, nor to émigrés who I now and then came into contact with.

Why had the Soviet authorities approached me in this way? Could it have been due to my letter to Ambassador Harriman? Maybe enquiries by the Russians had revealed that I had important connections in Italy and also in the USA. But, with my father and family (what had happened to them?) in Dresden, now run by the Russians, and with Italy in a mess, past Italian contacts had perhaps much lower value. As for any US connections, the Soviets couldn't have cared less about America or President Roosevelt, and from the press and propaganda it emerged that among the Allies the person they considered to be their real enemy was Winston Churchill. It was possible that questioning of me and reported conversations might have highlighted my little sympathy for the British.

This, along with my international background and education and my declared sympathy towards the Russian people, was perhaps what may have convinced the Soviets that I could be a useful element for them. But these were only possibilities, and not enough to put my mind at rest regarding their offer of a high position in an international organisation in which the USSR presumed it would play a major role.

Easy, my friend, I told myself. Let's play the moment. I was still a POW and would continue to evaluate the attitude of the Soviets towards me. In the meantime, I would keep my eyes open for the possibility of escape. I agreed with the saying *"Timeo Danaos et dona ferentes"* (beware of Greeks bearing gifts) but applied it to the Soviets, from whom nothing good could be expected. On the other hand, I would keep to my promise and avoid showing the most minimal sympathy towards Communism, especially now that this course had the blessing of the highest NKVD authority.

My conclusion was that I would play them at their own game and deceive them. I would escape when and if possible. As much as I liked the Russian people, I could never become a friend of the Soviet system and of an ideology that went so profoundly against everything I felt. That was the end of my reflections.

An example of how that system worked was evident when my sister tried, in 1944, to find out what had happened to me. Her brother-in-law, an adjutant to Gen Wavell in Africa, asked a British

MP friend for help. The MP wrote to the British ambassador in Moscow, Sir Archibald Kerr, asking him to enquire whether a certain Ferrante di Ruffano, an Italian officer, were dead or alive. Sir Archibald forwarded the enquiry to his Italian counterpart in Moscow, Ambassador Quaroni. It is only in 1947, in New York, that I had the chance to read the reply from Quaroni to Kerr. This stated that "…Capt Ferrante di Ruffano is not recorded among the prisoners of war. The lists here are very up to date. From what I gather, there were many snow storms where he was last seen and I was not able to learn more about the circumstances of his death." On this reply, a handwritten note from Ambassador Kerr reads: "Dear Chips – Alas! This is what I feared. Archibald, October 5, 1944." Yet, at that time I had recently left Camp 27A and had been to Moscow. The Soviet authorities knew only too well where I was, as they were also aware of the names and whereabouts of every other POW officer under investigation. The failure of that enquiry was due to the Soviet authorities, who intentionally denied any knowledge of me. My family was told I was still alive only when I managed to contact them after my repatriation in 1946.[31]

REGAINING STRENGTH

AT SUZDAL, I CHECKED that my notes were still hidden in the infirmary. A few other senior officers had joined us, and I found to my relief that nettle soup was no longer on the menu. Once, we were given whale meat, just a few grams, but it was excellent. When in the baths I noticed that my colleagues were looking fitter. I was amazed to see that Lieut Zan now had eight "breasts".

We enjoyed football games in the courtyard, where Capt Capone, a very Neapolitan character, proved to be an ace. I thought about teaching deck tennis but quickly remembered that I was disabled and must outwardly remain so. That said, if I tried to walk in the dark I lost my balance and everything appeared upside down. If I did escape and we moved only at night, how could I possibly keep up? I needed to get back into shape, as other friends of mine were doing.

During the summer I joined a work party to pick potatoes. After reaching the field, we stopped to rest among vandalised tombs in a cemetery near an isolated little church, now used as a vegetable depot. In the field nearby women and children were busy picking carrots. Two of the women came to us and one noticed the little medal of the Virgin hanging on a piece of string from my neck. It was the one given to me on that terrible train journey by my companion who died and whose name I had forgotten.

"Now I see why you survived," she said. "They have taken away religion from us. Our children have destroyed this cemetery and our men have all died. *Kak muchi umierli* (they died like flies), because they no longer had God."

I replied that at least they could eat what they picked in the field. And she said: "We have strict orders not to eat anything we pick from the field, not one potato or carrot. The children would denounce us to the kommissar. We just receive our daily rations." We felt sorry for these poor, friendly women. In the evening, we returned to Camp 160, our pockets filled with potatoes.

The doctors finally authorised me to go to work in the woods. Camino had some time ago informed me that his group cut down trees, took them to the sawmill and in the evening they received a double ration of bread, 600 grams! I could see how he had grown physically stronger. In August, I finally joined them.

We left on an old truck, escorted by armed guards. One of them was so thin and pale we called him Death and his son, also a guard at 160, naturally became known as Son of Death. When we arrived in the woods we were divided into groups of three, with each group provided with a double-handed saw and a thick rope.

With another POW, I was assigned a lighter task: we had to manufacture flat strips of wood, probably to be used in a textile factory. We were given a saw, two hatchets and a plane placed on a metal sheet on a tripod. The idea was to find straight young birch trees, remove the leaves and branches and cut them into 20cm sections (just over 6 inches) then, with the hatchets, cut them into strips about 4cm thick, before planing them. The hatchets were very sharp and we quickly learnt how to use them well. Our quota was 2000 pieces a day, however, and it remained beyond us so we never received our double rations.

A hidden bonus was that in the forest we were able to pick many mushrooms of every kind, although we didn't know which ones were edible. We avoided those with a fringe as they were reputed to be poisonous. In the evenings, near the shed where we slept, we used to boil them in a large tin and they reminded me of eating steak. We also ate wild berries. Yet, despite the improved diet, we remained hungry. I also found a small mirror and nail scissors lost in the shed by another POW.

I learned that our group had been assigned to work on the foundations of a railway route, where the Trans-Siberian line was to branch off. We needed to cut large trees and hoist the trunks onto our shoulders to take them to where the route had already been cut through. Again, I was excluded from this work, even though I enjoyed wielding an axe, a skill I had learned long ago in the USA.

The few locals we saw told us that it was severely prohibited to exceed "the norm", even for fire wood, where all that was allowed was 1kg per person, despite being in the middle of a forest. "But how is this possible?" we asked. The reply: "Obviously we exceed the quota, but it remains a danger that we might be discovered and forced to emigrate." There was a general fear of ending up in Siberia and working in the mines.

I still wore my *sciapka* to keep my head warm, even in summer. Nobody questioned it but it still had the magnetised needle stuck in it. One day, alone, I found a puddle and put my needle on a small leaf and watched it turning northwards, with great satisfaction. What a shame that I had found nobody else to plan an escape with me.

Speaking to an elderly Russian guard, I learned that the bark of young birch trees was good to eat when boiled and full of nutrients. The partisans had fed off it, together with many others who had found themselves without food. Good to know.

At the beginning of September a small group of us came back to Suzdal, the stronger ones being left in the forest to finish the work. Insistent voices predicted our imminent return to Italy, but we did not dare believe them. Too often in the past our hopes had been raised.

On the news sheet edited by the émigrés, *l'Alba*, as well as the usual articles denigrating Fascism, the monarchy, the Pope, religion and the army they had fought for, messages started to appear from the families of POWs, sent via Radio Moscow. How had they been informed that their loved ones were still alive? We discovered that these messages were being sent to the "enlightened ones" of the Anti-Fascist School.

Here at Suzdal, some time before we had found in the cupboard of an Italian émigré a large pile of postcards that we had written over a period of time. They had obviously been intercepted and never forwarded. The camp authorities couldn't care less about our loved ones being reassured. All they were interested in was the names of the POWs and to which addresses they were trying to write. After this incident, we had collectively decided to stop writing home.

The discovery that our mail had never been sent home but had been intercepted by the State Police with the connivance of the émigrés came as a nasty shock. Despite the absence of replies, they had given us an illusion of hope. This only stiffened my resolve not to give in. I was also mindful of how Tenente Italo Stagno, after speaking up for our fallen comrades who had disappeared, was sentenced to forced labour in Siberia. So, in September 1945, I acted, despite the risk of retribution from the Soviets. I stole one of the Soviet flags that fluttered around the camp following victory over the Germans and tore off a piece, as large as a handkerchief. Then, from the lining of a German overcoat, I cut a rectangle of green material. Lastly, from my bedsheet I took a piece of white fabric. I then sewed the pieces together and, in the central white part, with red and blue crayons I drew the cross of the royal house of Savoy, above which I added the crown. This was our flag for which we had fought and shed our blood. I rolled it tightly around a small branch from one of the bushes in the camp and at first put it in my bag. But I needed to conceal it better from the guards, so I buried it with my notes in the infirmary, waiting for the moment of departure when I might smuggle it out.

We were joined by the German generals whom I had met at the villa. I noted that many of them had put the Wehrmacht eagle back on their uniforms. Maybe this was because they were under less stress. However, a few days later, they had, once again, all removed their eagles. I couldn't help but notice the disappointment and shame on the faces of junior German officers whom I had befriended on seeing their superiors behave so shamelessly. We were informed that Von Paulus, commander of the 6th Army at Stalingrad, was under pressure and that his colleague Gen Von Seidlitz had founded the *Freies Deutschland* group, under the auspices of the USSR Communist Party. However, we had no news of Gen Artur Schmidt, who was probably being still kept away because of his pride and his obstinate failure to accept Soviet propaganda.

TRAIN CRASH

DURING THE SECOND HALF of September 1945 I was advised by Pio Paolozzi that the *Kommandatura* had informed him that he was about to leave Suzdal, but he was saddened by the fact that his brother Toio would not go with him. Pio was to be accompanied by five other prisoners and I was one of them. Where were we going? We had no idea. Coming with us were Lieut Mare, elderly and infirm, and Lieut Palmieri, unhinged after his repeated mock executions in the Lubjanka. I cannot remember the names of the others.[32]

Upon learning the news of my departure, I realised that it was unlikely I would return to Suzdal. Just before leaving, I went to the infirmary, ostensibly for a last dose of pills, but in reality to recover my notes from their hiding place. Leaving my bag with my few earthly possessions at the door, I retrieved my records and managed to add them to the bag, without being detected. I also took the tightly rolled little flag, which I held with my walking stick. Then I went to receive my pills. The moment had come to leave and to risk everything. Had they found the records in my bag, or the flag, I would not have left Russia, but ... *audaces fortuna iuvat*. I called the guard to carry out the customary personal search. He pronounced me clean. Taking a deep breath, I walked out of the infirmary and picked up my bag as if it were the most natural thing in the world. No one shouted after me. I had made it.

The train left, heading west towards Moscow. For a few moments, I feared we might be going to the Lubjanka. We reached Moscow but, when the train stopped, we had to stay on board, although we had permission to leave our carriage to get *tipiatok* (boiling water) from taps along the tracks. We all had our individual mess tins and they gave us *sachari* (salted biscuits), salted raw fish and a bucket of *ciai*. We stayed there for four days and at night were locked into our carriage. What was happening?

Other carriages were coupled to our train, mostly from oriental Russia and full of wounded German POWs. When we finally pulled out, our train had become very long and included more than 100 carriages, although in Russia this was not unusual. Some Germans started to become sick, as they had deliberately poisoned themselves by drinking boiled tobacco to become unable to work and be repatriated sooner. This claimed quite a few fatalities, however, and during the numerous stops we had to take the dead from the carriages and throw them down the rail embankment. This satisfied the living though who could eat their rations.

The further west we travelled, the more we started to hope that we would end up maybe not in Italy, but in a lager in Poland or Prussia. We reached Warsaw and were in the middle of another long stop when another train pulled up opposite ours. Its doors remained locked. It was full of Russians who had fought with the Germans and were being repatriated as prisoners. They all seemed depressed. According to our guards, the authorities feared that, on coming back, these men would start to conduct counter-propaganda, as they had experienced a level of culture that Stalinism had always denied. So they were not going home, but were heading for Siberia or central Asia to disappear and be forgotten.

One evening, the train had stopped and our Russian guards were outside, drunk on vodka, with us locked into our cattle carriages, when a tremendous jolt heaped us all on top of one another. Another train had arrived at speed and rammed into us. The last three carriages were wrecked, and many had been killed or wounded. The guards opened our carriages and yelled at us to help evacuate the destroyed carriages. No Italians were on board, only Germans and a few Romanians and Hungarians. I don't know what happened to the wounded, but the order was given not to throw the dead onto the embankment – the normal procedure with dead POWs – but to take them quickly and discreetly into the forest and to bury them. I helped and with colleagues pulled bodies under the trees. We dug shallow graves with bare hands. For two of the corpses I had time to make two small crosses, with string and branches. I planted these on their graves. With a piece of pencil and some paper from a colleague, I wrote: *"Hier liegt ein Deutscher Soldat"*. We should be in Germany by now, I said to myself. One day, they will be found.

The destroyed carriages had been uncoupled and we reboarded our train, continuing as if nothing had happened. We had been lucky because our carriage was near the locomotive, yet we were not affected by what had happened, or by the fate of the wounded. While the POWs who had been captured recently had not lived through the horrors imposed on us by the Soviets and were now overcome with horror, the disaster left us indifferent. We had become removed from any kind of emotion or feeling.

When we reached Pozdan, Pio Paolozzi and I had a disagreement. Among the Italian POWs on the train I was the highest-ranking officer and de facto became responsible for our group. Pio asked me to delegate command to him, as he knew Russian, but I said that, as we were now closer to home, it was my wish to occupy the position that was rightfully mine. Our friendship abruptly came to an end and Pio vanished in one of the stations on the way. I later learned that he was sent to Berlin and made his way back separately to Italy. Pio's brother Toio also made it back to Italy and we remained good friends.

A GERMAN CAMP

WE REACHED FRANKFURT-AM-ODER, in what became East Germany, and were directed to Lager NKVD 69. I was with about 80 Italians soldiers and three officers in one hut, the Germans occupied another, while the French, Dutch and Belgians who had fought with the Wehrmacht were in a third. We remained here until 2nd January 1946.

The Russians considered me as commandant of the Italians, all of us wounded or frail. I still needed my walking stick to steady myself in the dark. I had difficulty believing that we were going to be repatriated. After all that had happened, I had acquired some of the Russian mentality, and had become deeply fatalistic. Nothing surprised me. I noticed that rations had become abundant. The Russians wanted to fatten us up and return some of our individuality, possibly to make us more presentable on repatriation. That may have been the main reason for keeping us here all this time.

As much propaganda as ever continued with the same meetings on Communism and Anti-Fascism, but no demands were placed on the Italians. There were about 80 of us Italians, all in a poor state or badly wounded, led by only four officers. I reported daily that everyone was present, on whom in my group had been referred to the infirmary, and also ensured that the men had enough rations. That was it and otherwise the Russians left us alone. As head of my group, I was also given a *fufaika* (anorak) for the cold, and new shirts.

Among the POWs were many who had fought on the second front, against the Anglo-Americans in Normandy, before they were sent to try to stop the Russian advance. Without exception, they said the landing in France had cost the Allies an enormous number of men, even though their clear superiority of materiel and troops had eventually prevailed.

We started to guess what was happening in Italy. (We no longer received *l'Alba* so, when I went to the toilet, I used pages from Stalin's *Questions on Leninism*. The library was well stocked and, in this instance, Stalin came in useful.) And the long weeks spent at Camp 69 gave me time to give serious thought to my situation and to try to make sense of what was happening around me. I had volunteered to fight this war, always on the front line, faithful to deep-rooted ideals matured from infancy in the long years when living abroad with my family. As a family, we were proud to represent this marvellous Italy that Mussolini had presented to the world, a small nation noticed and sometimes envied by richer countries for the progress and successes achieved over two decades. Churchill, a few months before the start of the war, had described Mussolini as "the greatest living legislator who had shown to the world how to resist the onslaught of Socialism, indicating through the Fascist regime the path that a nation enjoying courageous leadership could follow."

By Socialism, Churchill, of course, meant Communism, which he had opposed from the first. We followed suit, assisting Franco in the Spanish Civil War and then fighting on the Russian front. Until 1937 all our military endeavours had been successful, but the campaigns in Africa, Albania-Greece and Russia had collectively been an unmitigated disaster, as I had borne witness. I felt that the Allies – British, American or Russian – were as one and, taken individually as combatants, could not begin to match us. The previous successes, as my father often commented, were not due to the politicians surrounding Mussolini, but to the initiatives of the Duce himself, who, even if brilliant, had to rely on incompetent ministers and generals. It was they who eventually encouraged him on the road to disaster.

Poor Duce, in the purity of your belief in a powerful Italy, you placed your trust in megalomaniacs such as Badoglio and Ciano, to the detriment of the nation. To the eyes of the world, the

Italian betrayal, even more than the reputation of incompetence, was bound to weigh heavily and for a long time. Such were my thoughts at that time.

I was also amazed still to be alive. If I could miraculously survive this inhuman imprisonment I would have little or nothing in common with the man I had been, transformed and tempered by what I had endured: Death Gorge in Albania, full of bodies without limbs, a head here, a leg there, crows pecking at corpses on our forced march in Greece, the mortal panic during the sinking of the *Galilea*, firefights on the Don and those first months of captivity when I never renounced my principles. Death, mutilation, limbs decomposing with gangrene, the suffering of people close to me – all had leached the feelings of a normal man from me. I had become incapable of real emotion.

I had experienced deep hunger and thirst and the painful reaction of my body to them. I could not feel any hate toward the soldiers who fought against us, who killed us to fulfil their duty and to survive, nor could I hate the civilian population, who were everywhere the same. I had, however, come to hate politicians and the countries, Britain and the US, that had helped Communism, our real enemy. I sometimes repeated to myself the verses I had written from a poetry book read in Suzdal, signing it under the pseudonym Longfellow:

Oh God,
Grant me the force of Remembering
These moments that never pass;
Grant me the power of detesting
This system that is a poison to us.
Grant me the future of Revenging
These horrors that I've lived up to – indeed
And grant me, oh God, in Remaining
The man which I've always been:
True to himself – to his Country,
To his people and also to his creed!

These words, along with the verse of Virgil glimpsed in the underground jail at Krasnojegorsk – "Arise from my bones, o avenger, whoever you may be", constituted my strongest feelings at the time: hate and revenge.

Towards the end of December 1945 we heard that repatriation was imminent and everyone was sent to the camp depot to change their clothes. On 2nd January 1946 the official departure order arrived. Imitating the French, Belgians and Dutch I assembled my Italian contingent just outside the main gate, leaving the sick behind to be repatriated at a later date. The camp commandant, a Russian colonel, came to inspect each contingent and, on reaching the Germans, cordially shook the hand of its commander.

When he reached us, and in response to my salute, he glared at me and said: *"Vi Italianski!"* (you Italians), then spat at my feet. Surprised, I replied: *"Spassiba"* (thank you) and looked straight back at him. In that moment, I saw in his eyes the opinion that the world now had of us Italians. I was shaken by this and would have liked to have replied: "...but out on the battlefield we Alpini decimated you."

That was the last military salute I received.

We boarded another train. The officers now occupied compartments, while the soldiers still travelled cattle class. We were travelling south, dressed as Russian peasants. As the head of my contingent, I sported a sleeve-band saying *Vertreter Italiener* (Italian representative). We were excited, but the train wasted a lot of time dawdling at stations or in open countryside.

Two Russians were in our compartment. They were dressed as civilians, but who could tell with the Soviets? They told us that the war had been won by the Russians and that the USA and Britain had waited for the Germans to be worn down on the eastern front before launching their attack in Normandy. We agreed with them and that the end had begun with Stalingrad, and only culminated with the atom bomb on Hiroshima. "But rest assured", they added, "we will also soon have atomic weapons too." I said this was obvious, as Soviet methods and knowledge would easily prevail over that of the Anglo-Saxons.

Three days later we reached Hof, near the border between Russian- and British-occupied Germany. We stopped again at the border and remained there, eating *kasha,* raw fish, *sachari* and *ciai* and anxiously waiting for something to happen. The British were negotiating seriously with the Russians, who were talking about sending us back east. The British wanted the train to proceed. POWs of other nationalities were gradually moved elsewhere until only us Italians were left on board. Our Russian fellow-travellers had also vanished. The debate between the British and Russians became more heated and argumentative. We started to fear being sent back to a Soviet camp and even began to make plans to escape.

Finally, on 9th January, we were delivered into British custody and were immediately escorted to a large depot to be fumigated against parasites. Our bodies and clothes were covered in sulphur. Two days later we arrived in Munich, in the American Zone. I presented myself to the office of the American officer in charge and was escorted to a small office where a captain sat with his feet up on the table. When I reported on my contingent he asked me, in perfect Italian, to take a seat. He was Italian, but in the US Army! At this point, I started to speak to him in English and he became friendlier, informing me that we would continue the journey and that I could travel in the locomotive and eat better. I moved up to the locomotive with three US soldiers and was given a tin of meat, cigarettes, and chocolate: a K-ration. It was fantastic. We reached Innsbruck in Austria and I rejoined my colleagues back in my carriage.

In the afternoon of the 11th January, we crossed the Brenner Pass and arrived on Italian soil.

BACK IN ITALY

WE WERE ALL TOLD to remain on board, but the head of the convoy was requested. I identified myself and asked for immediate assistance for the many wounded on board. An ambulance arrived but I was the only person allowed off the train. I was taken to Merano, where an American field hospital had been set up at the Hotel Emma. I was taken to a room with a bed, sheets, pillows and blankets. I undressed and got into bed, where I was given an orange. I ate it voraciously, pips included, and skin. The nurse was amazed, called her colleagues and brought me another orange, which I devoured similarly. I was no longer used to similar luxuries, however, and next morning they found me asleep under the bed, snugly wrapped in my blanket.

Over the following days I was properly examined by an excellent military doctor and noticed that the severely wounded on my train were also being cared for at the hospital. A soldier from Avellino had both his legs amputated. I met an army chaplain, Don

Amoroso, but didn't think much of him. The Red Cross gave me some shaving equipment, a tooth brush, a military jacket, belt and some good shoes.

One morning I was told that they had decided to operate on me. The doctor said that the shrapnel was at the back of the head, next to the cerebellum and that he would operate without anaesthetic. I was asked to lie on my stomach on the operating table, where my ankles, mid-riff and right wrist were tied. My left arm was left free. The doctor called over a good-looking nurse and asked her to sit in front of me. "Look, she's beautiful, isn't she? Now place your free hand on her thigh. I will not hurt you, but you must remain silent. Should you experience any pain, just squeeze her thigh, she will speak for you." And so it went. The pain that stung when the suture was applied was more than compensated for by my caressing of the thigh… I remained silent. After the operation I was given the shrapnel as a memento.

Since arriving at the hospital I had made every effort to locate my family, to tell them I was wounded, but alive and back. I wrote to the Red Cross, to my grandparents in Naples, to the Foreign Ministry, to my Jesuit uncle in Livorno. "Who is still alive? Where are you?"

One morning I received a visit from a senior diplomat, Baron Destrobel, who owned a villa in the area. At the ministry they called him the Panzer Baron, because he spoke German and had an imposing stomach. Destrobel had a letter from my father, informing me that, all things considered, the family were fine. He was still unable to reach me by telephone, but would come to visit as soon as the travel conditions and weather permitted.

During my stay in Merano, I undid the lining of my coat and retrieved all those cigarette papers and loose notebook pages that I had patiently compiled and hidden during my stay in the camps. I started to write down all the names of colleagues still in Soviet hands, those whom I had seen when they were still alive but I also included the dead, listing them by order of unit. I sent the completed lists to the War Ministry in Rome, but also informed the press and radio of colleagues I had left in Suzdal.

As the news spread, I started to receive an enormous number of visits from families of military personnel who had not made it back from Russia. Those still numbered well over 100,000. Their relatives came to me, asking for news of sons, husbands and close family members. I remember having to inform two mothers, each with two sons on the Russian front, that their sons had died in prison camps. One diplomat had come back from Argentina to enquire about his brother, who was with me on the front, and where he had died of dysentery. It was a painful duty, but a necessary one.

I wrote an article that was quickly published in the *Gazzettino Veneto*, openly accusing the Italian émigré Togliatti and Soviet authorities of our ill-treatment. These accusations were confirmed by all my colleagues after they were repatriated. I later learned that the Soviets reacted badly to my article. Another leading émigré, Commissar Robotti, referring to Italian POWs still in Russian custody, said that one of their number, generously freed, had repaid them by denigrating the Soviet system. "This is proof that none of you deserve to go back to Italy," He said. It was divulged that I was the culprit and I was roundly cursed.

During my convalescence in hospital I started to heal physically, but not enough for my mind to regain a sense of normality. A nurse became infatuated with me. She used to call me King-Kong and wanted me to father her child. Another girl came to visit me and fell in love, later writing me one of the most beautiful love letters I have ever received. This all felt very odd, because at the time my face was distorted and I looked pretty terrible.

Lucia, the girl I was in love with when I left for the Russian front, sent me a cable then wrote, but her letter never arrived. Finally, with a sadness I cannot begin to describe, I decided to end our relationship. We were practically engaged and she had waited for me. But I had become another person, physically and mentally. Nothing affected me and I felt dead to all feeling and emotion. It would not have been fair on her.

During those days in Merano I heard of what had happened in Italy, the destruction, the civil war from 1943 to 1945, the opprobrium of Mussolini, shot and hanged by the feet, and of the Fascists who had so rapidly converted to anti-Fascism. I wondered which of my acquaintances had not become a turncoat, who would I be able to trust and respect as a friend?

I left Merano in an American Jeep with a girl who asserted that she was American, despite barely being able to speak a few words of English. I didn't know whether to despise or pity her. We reached Milan, where I spent the night with Gen Marras, a former military attaché to Berlin, and left for Rome early the following morning, on an old, open truck full of people and household furnishings. I sat quietly in a corner, wearing my warm *fufaika* with the *sciapka* on my head. I had discarded my walking stick and the headaches were becoming rarer, but I still lost my balance in the dark.

We drove through areas where the war had left chaos and destruction, but I barely saw them. I was immunised. We arrived in Rome and stopped in front of the Coliseum. The weather was sunny. In Piazza St Peter I finally saw my father and we hugged. My family were safe and well. We had lost everything but had all survived the war. My Father was the consul-general in Dresden in 1943 when Italy changed sides. The Germans had asked him to choose between the new republican Fascist government in northern Italy or remain faithful to the Kingdom of Italy, which had switched sides to the Allies. My father chose to remain faithful to the King and the family was deported to northern Italy. All our possessions were left in Dresden and obliterated by the RAF.

With the end of the war and Italy still in chaos, my father managed to travel to Rome and present himself to the ministry to be reintegrated in the Diplomatic Service. He was appointed head of the Italian legation in Venezuela and asked me what I intended to do, proposing that I should go with him to Caracas. I replied that I had come back as a different person and didn't have any idea of what the future could hold for me.

My father had also been in contact with HRH Prince Umberto, the Italian interim head of state who briefly became King Umberto II. The Prince had requested a meeting with me and I duly presented myself, giving him a detailed report on my period as a POW in Russia. He decorated me personally (*Motu Proprio*) and I was later offered the honour of becoming Grand Chancellor of the Order of the Italian Crown, an honour I accepted[33].

However, the time in Rome became progressively more depressing. I spent two days going between the military district and the hospital, where the colonel in charge insisted that I sign a statement that I had received "a small wound to the face". The NCO dealing with my file approached me for a favour which I was unable to grant; he then became totally disinterested and made several errors in recording dates and facts in my personal notes. Disgusted, I left.

I went to stay for a couple of days with my great-uncle, who was more senile than I remembered. I took the opportunity to discard some of the souvenirs I had brought back from France and Greece: hand-grenades I had taken apart to use as cigarette holders, two mortar bombs without their explosive (we had used it to go fishing in the Gulf of Istmia), the barrel of a machine-gun taken at Fort Conchetas. I had stopped caring about all of that.

Above all, I found it impossible to accept the fact that all those people who had enthusiastically acclaimed Fascism, loudly calling for entry into a war that proved an unmitigated disaster, had prudently remained at home and were now equally enthusiastic for the Allies. I vividly recalled the suffering of our men, dying for their country without warm clothing, food and ammunition and contrasted it to this new attitude around me.

I learned about the German reprisals after 32 of their men were killed by a bomb in Via Rasella in Rome. They had rounded up over 300 Italian hostages and shot them. But, had you been in the Germans' shoes, what would you have done?

I also remembered my aunt and some family friends, who were openly pro-British in 1939, and the Fascist government had done nothing against them.

And now we had several government ministers, who had actively betrayed their country's armed forces (Togliatti had caused the disappearance of thousands of Italian POWs in Russia), installed with the blessing of the Allies as the reward for their betrayal.

The people around me seemed resigned: "Dear Toni, after all, we are the losers and we must…" "No," I replied, "You are the losers. I never gave up." What shitty people had the Italians become, without backbone, slaves to the Americans, the Russians and the British. What would future generations think of us who, in the previous 20 years, had been admired and respected because of the achievements of the "hateful Fascist regime"?

8: AFTERMATH

A CCEPTING FATHER'S OFFER to go with the family to Venezuela via the USA, I left Rome with him for the port of Naples, to embark for New York. In Naples I met my mother and the rest of my family: Vanni, my teenage brother, who had lost two fingers when playing with an unexploded projectile, and the youngest, Bobby, who was ill due to severe vitamin deficiency. My aunt Zia Anna and the cousins were well, even if they too had lost everything.

We sailed from Naples on 27th February 1946 on a Liberty Ship. Father had bought some clothes with money he had borrowed. All my pre-war clothes had been given to Vanni as I had been presumed dead, but I still had my POW clothes and they were enough for me. Everyone on board was kind, the food both excellent and abundant. The sea was rough for most of the crossing, which reminded me of my own shipwreck four years before. I kept the memory to myself.

After 10 days we reached the US coast near Norfolk, Virginia, where the ship became lodged on a sand bank, probably because the crew had been drinking heavily. We arrived in New York on 19th March and went to stay in the beautiful house of my maternal great-uncle, John Henry Hammond, in Manhattan.

Uncle John's wife, Emily Vanderbilt, of the US dynasty, headed the international Moral Rearmament movement. Born in the immorality of war, this was an effort to regain a sense of the morality that mankind had seemed to have lost. Aunt Emily loved me and, even when I refused to join her movement, referred me to the best doctors, surgeons and dentists to enable me fully to recover. Without my knowledge, she paid all the bills.

I was invited through my cousins Ogden and Louie Starr to make a speech at the Naval Academy in Annapolis, Maryland, and at the Rotary International club in Newark, New Jersey. I gave the speeches still dressed as a *mugik* (Russian peasant) and openly criticised the Americans' Soviet ally: "They are your real enemy and you know it," I said. I also strongly rebuked some US Air Force officers, who had said that they had shot any captured

Japanese. They justified this by saying: "They are not humans, they are animals." My response was that if POWs were protected by international law, why didn't US servicemen recognise this?

On 2nd June 1946, the Allies imposed a referendum in Italy in which Italians had to vote on fundamental institutional changes. The date was chosen because many military personnel abroad – a large majority of whom favoured the monarchy – would not be repatriated in time to participate. In addition, any Italian who had fought against the Allies in 1943 to 1945 could not take part. I was therefore excluded from this referendum and was never officially contacted so the reason could be explained. I have refused to participate to this day in any Italian elections.

I left New York to join my father in Venezuela. There I found a job working for the Texas Oil Company in the state of Guarico South, close to the Orinoco river. Then it was still a wild and primitive region. However, despite earning a good salary, after a few months I decided to return to New York to find a job. The reason was that, during my first stay in New York, I had met Sunny, who was to become my wife and with whom I went on to have three children. But finding a job in the US proved difficult and initially everyone turned me down: "You are an enemy, you fought against the Allies," they said. I did not give up and eventually found a job with American Export Lines at a minimal salary, $12.72 a week, despite my languages and university degree. When I married Sunny in 1947, my salary was increased to $18.50 per week.

A few months after my second arrival in New York I was contacted by a new organisation. It called itself the Central Intelligence Agency. Until the end of the war, the Soviet Union's enormous contribution towards the defeat of the Axis had been admired. But with the end of hostilities and the advance of Communism in central Europe, Western governments started to feel apprehensive. The US decided to reorganise its secret service, the OSS, renaming it and giving it additional resources to counter the advance of Communism. The CIA was born.

I had become aware that I had been under observation for some time, but in an amateurish way. Finally, the agency decided to approach me with an offer of employment. However, after my POW experience and the hard lessons learned from the Soviet State Security Service, this all seemed like a game to me. The Americans appeared childish and did not seem to take anything seriously.

Their offer did feature one noteworthy detail – the promise of a permanent job with a good salary. It was almost too good to be true. However, another important issue became clear: joining the CIA might hand me the chance to put a spoke in the wheels of advancing Communism and repay the Soviets for the treatment inflicted on Italian POWs. I would certainly be unable to achieve this in Italy: the monarchy had been abolished and, with no strong government, the new anti-Fascist Italian republic seemed powerless to hold in check an ever stronger Italian Communist Party, which was being helped by Moscow.

I agreed to join. However, before becoming part of the agency, I had to undergo a lie detector test, to ensure if I could be trusted. My feelings and beliefs had not changed, but I agreed enthusiastically to answer all questions put to me. It is important to know, however, that I presented myself at the test with a small photograph of Benito Mussolini in my pocket. I answered the many questions that aimed to ascertain my political feelings and beliefs – and passed with flying colours. After this experience and a long period of indoctrination and training, I was given US citizenship by a federal magistrate, another condition of employment. It was 1951.

Now employed by the CIA, but outwardly still working for American Export Lines, I was posted to Genoa as assistant to the director general for Europe. The job carried a salary of $5,000 a year, net of tax and with all expenses paid. From 1951 to 1958 I worked first in Genoa, then in Rome with the aim of helping to neutralise the advance of Communism.

In 1953 Josef Stalin, secretary of the Communist Party of the USSR and dictator of the Soviet Union, died. Although officially an American, I had kept in contact with my Alpini who had been Russian POWs. Stalin's demise and our luck in being alive needed celebrating and I organised a great party at Portofino, on the Italian Riviera near Genoa. On my way to Portofino and before boarding the overnight train I bought some fish, to be served salted to my former POW colleagues, as a reminder of the same food we had received in the camps. It was a warm night and the train was packed. By the time we arrived, the stench from the fish could no longer be ignored, but, on the bright side, my compartment had emptied. At the end of our meal, a large cake featuring a huge pair of moustachios arrived at the table.[34]

Suddenly, in 1958, I was summoned by my superior, William Colby (who went on to become head of the CIA). He told me the agency no longer needed my services. With this, I was given two weeks' notice, the usual period given by US companies when dismissing personnel. I was told that the Communist threat in Italy had lessened, that the CIA was going to be reorganised and the initial promise of a permanent job no longer counted. I was married, with two children, had worked well and yet here I was without a job.

Looking back, the experience of working for the CIA just after the war was very interesting, an experience that one day I would have pleasure in recalling separately. However, I was disgusted at being let go in this way. Back in 1951 I had received US citizenship, so now I decided to renounce it. Within the year, I presented myself to the US consulate-general in Rome, where I asked for a written statement confirming that I was no longer a US citizen. This move, at a time when everyone was trying to obtain American citizenship, was unheard of and offensive to the US government.

Luck, however, had not abandoned me. In that same year, I managed to find a position in Belgium with Euratom, the Atomic Agency of the newly formed Common Market, which had been established through the Treaty of Rome the year before. At the beginning of 1959 my family and I moved to Brussels, where I still live.

I still remember that Romanian POW who, in 1943 in Vietluskaja concentration camp on the edge of Siberia, offered to foretell my future in exchange for a portion of my tobacco. I was then still in a poor state, hobbling with the help of two sticks and I had a gaping hole in my head. He read my hand and, ignoring my incredulity, said that I would survive, be repatriated, regain my health, have three children and lead a long and interesting life. How I would love to give him another portion of my tobacco.

EPILOGUE:
THE TOLL OF WAR

*This description of life in a Russian POW camp was written by my
friend and fellow prisoner Lieut Carlo Vicentini. Although he was
describing what he experienced living outside of Camp 160
working as a painter for the people of Suzdal, it is an eloquent
portrait of our life worth quoting in full.*[35]

T HE MAN WHO RETURNS from war is not the same as he
was before. He is another individual. His personality,
especially if he is very young, which is generally the case,
becomes changed utterly. He departs motivated by ideals, by
enthusiasm, by a spirit of adventure, by an ambition to do
something deserving commendation. He departs because of
solidarity, so as not to feel cowardly. He would be ashamed to
remain at home while friends, relatives and married acquaintances
go to the front. He departs because he considers it is a duty from
which he cannot withdraw. Some also, of course, go to war furious
and perplexed because they have been compelled to. But almost all
are repaid with the same token: disillusionment.

War is a ruthless sledgehammer that crushes and annihilates
all individuality, transforming men into robots from which
anything may be taken. It is a huge grinding machine, pulverising
the strongest characters, bending the most stubborn, nullifying any
will to protest. Indifferent to physical, moral and sentimental needs,
it demolishes myths and ideals, destroys convictions, overturns
habits and provokes loss of compassion, decency and honesty. It
develops only one talent: unresisting acquiescence.

A soldier learns to march for days on end, not knowing where
he is being sent, and to rest on other days in impossible places. He
is often ordered to leave immediately, even at night and in pouring
rain, and to return to where he started from. He is driven to
exhaustion after being required to organise himself in a designated

position, only to be ordered the next day to hand it over to another unit.

He thinks he has a right to eat at least once a day, but learns to skip his meals, to swallow cold and disgusting food in haste or in a dust storm, in mud or when a blizzard blows the scraps off his spoon. He learns to stay awake when he is collapsing with tiredness and to sleep standing as his mules do; to live for days and nights with his clothing soaked by rain. He must obey incompetent, unjust and frightened superiors. He must fight even when he's terrified, when he knows that the possibility of coming out alive is minimal. If he figures out a thousand ways how not to be captured or killed, he knows that the moment could come as soon as he is taken.

Death, mutilation and suffering surround him and happen every day. He loses his sense of tragedy and the emotions that move a normal man. He has learnt to kill, or rather to shoot at men for whom he feels no hatred, without thinking that, at that instant, he is killing them. He has learnt the difference between the two when he feels the horror engulf him if, by chance, he meets the eyes of the dying enemy.

Rarely is there a feeling of true hatred towards the enemy, although he may think he has such feeling when subjected to propaganda aimed at belittling a soldier. He usually goes to war with the same spirit he has for sport. He fights because he is proud, for his self-esteem. He will not admit that his adversary, even though cleverer and stronger, may overcome him – he does everything he can so as not to be defeated. He is nevertheless, capable of stubborn solidity, of determination, of generosity and sublime conduct, preferring not to submit, like many companions, to the belief that sacred principles such as love of homeland, of the binding character of an oath, of devotion to a sovereign, are nothing but empty rhetoric.

Then there is the man who sacrifices himself to motivate and draw in reluctant soldiers to resolve a hopelessly compromised situation. In doing so, he saves the lives of his companions. He is the true hero, rare if only, because of his self-sacrifice, his feat cannot be repeated. Public acknowledgement focuses on him to feed the myth that war is good and holy. Yet, such events are not always reported. Many heroes remain unknown to those who hand out medals.

I do not believe in the abolition of war. Human history teaches us that this is utopic. I wouldn't even want to discuss whether war can have better reasons, for those who want to justify it. I only wish to mention some of war's consequences on the unfortunates who are called to fight on the battlefield rather than from the rear lines or from general staff quarters.

If providence allows these soldiers home, they are what I call the *repatriated*. And among these is a special kind, those who add to their battle experience a period as a POW. Under any flag, this is far from being a pleasant experience. In some cases, it is worse than combat. And I do not exaggerate in maintaining that POWs in Russian hands in the past war were the most unfortunate of all, except for those who returned from there – these can be considered the most fortunate.

What became of these men who returned from the USSR after all they had witnessed, endured and suffered? How did they change?

Within a few months – because the initial phase in battle was most indelibly impressed on them – they will have acquired a perspective on life and values that few may ever expect to have, except perhaps for those who were saved from Nazi extermination camps. One must go back centuries to find experiences similar to theirs, perhaps to the barbarian invasions or the slave trade. The years after that initial, determining phase and the later return to normal life were never enough to cancel the Russian POWs character, his habits, tastes and attitudes, his very ways of thinking and doing.

Because I have to hand a sample of one of them – myself – I will try to trace his profile.

He is a man no longer capable of full emotion. No disaster, no massacre, no sorrowing event moves him. He has such abnormal terms of reference that any comparison is overwhelmed. Calamities, illnesses and grievous upsets affecting himself, or his family (his loss of feeling extends to those around him), are felt with distress and disappointment, but, crucially, without grief. He has learnt that loss has a profounder aspect.

He has a tolerant character. He is fatalistic, almost indifferent. He feels not depression if his home is robbed or his wallet lost, nor does he react as others do if his car is broken into, if red tape toys with him and makes him lose time, if deserved promotion, advancement in business or pension benefits fail to arrive, if his children do not blossom as he expects, or his holiday turns to ruin. He has absorbed from the Russians some of their fatalism. Like them, he has understood that it's not only pointless to oppose fate but to rail against it.

He is a man who does not get heated in discussion. Every topic bores him within moments. He gives no great credit to political, economic or moral pronouncements. He has learnt that everything is relative. The separation between good and bad, right and wrong, true and false is not clear-cut.

He is a man who has learned to resolve personally, with a minimum of technical knowledge and a little imagination, all the difficulties and inconveniences of daily life. He can work as a carpenter, mason, plumber, electrician, painter, blacksmith or gardener. He has learnt that, in dire need, he has unimagined resources.

He is a man who never complains of stomach ache, toothache or fever. He may have it, but that is all. Not a word comes from him after a bad cut, a burn, a sprained ankle. He is ashamed to show pain, to show any signs of suffering, even when he feels excruciating agony. Doctors theorise that this must be due to a lack of sensitivity, and that it is something to be envied. It is no more than modesty. When witness to so many severe wounds – stomachs ripped open, legs half torn off, faces mangled by explosive blasts, a chest become a sieve thanks to a fistful of splinters, extremities putrefied by frostbite, worms crawling whitely in flesh – but hearing no protest or despair, just a quiet moaning, he learns that pain has a magnitude beyond most men's ken.

He is a man who knows the meaning of hunger, who can read it in another man's eyes. He understands that "world hunger" can never be eliminated by charities. Food has become sacred to him, something that is sinful to waste. He leaves nothing on his plate even when he's full. He feels offended if leftovers are thrown out. He does not allow it – that food might have been used in so many ways the next day. He may be a gourmet, yet he will eat anything put before him. He cannot refuse too salty a dish, nor one that is half raw, overcooked or badly prepared.

He cannot discard meagre objects or throw anything away. Everything can become useful. An inch of cloth, a scrap of paper, a piece of string, a can or a nail were precious things in his past. It might seem a ridiculous habit of mind, but it remains something a Russian repatriate is incapable of abandoning.

He recalls that man will become an animal if subjected to enough strain, if tortured by circumstance. A man will arrive at eating his fellow man if forced by events, at killing a dying man for food if his instinct has told him that he must not eat the putrefying dead.

He is the product of exceptional circumstances. He cannot pretend to be an examplar. He refuses to teach anything. The world has its right to judge and classify him as it wishes.

For him, death is nothing, neither his own nor of those closest to him. He has witnessed too many bodies in the fields which the people thereabout saw as mere fertiliser for their land.

He knows he is happy. He is content with what life has to offer. He is content to be alive. He believes that every day that passes is a gift. His mind forever returns to the several thousand friends who ended their young days in a land, and for a cause, that was not really theirs.

NOTES

1 I lost track of Marchesi after Spain and didn't meet him until after the war when I saw him between 1957 and 1960 at the Ministry of Defence in Rome. His brilliant career had led him to becoming a Lieut-Gen and Chief of Staff of the Army. Our friendship continues today, although as his rank increased so did his weight.

[2] I met Sgt Vaona many years later in Belgium, in 1964, where he had moved to work as a miner in Limburg. He died in the 1970s.

[3] Mussolini's son-in-law and Foreign Minister from 1936-43.

[4] I still have the French flag. It hangs on the wall of my study.

[5] From the minutes of the meeting of 13th August 1940 between Mussolini, Foreign Minister Ciano and the chiefs of staff, where the decision to attack Greece was taken.

[6] *Porca naia*: no equivalent English expression, (literally "bloody conscription").

[7] The Arditi were assault troops formed of just a few men who, committed to extreme operations, launched themselves in the vanguard against the enemy, much as the San Marco battalion do for the Italian navy.

[8] Duchessa Badoglio was the wife of Gen Pietro Badoglio, one of the leaders of the Italian army at the end of the First World War. He became a Field Marshal and in 1943, on the downfall of Mussolini, turned against Fascism and was instrumental in Italy switching from the Axis to the Allies.

[9] For ease of description, Positions are located according to their elevation above sea level.

[10] According to German documents printed by the Allies. 12th series, 1956.

[11] Years later, in 1970, visiting the headquarters of the Associazione Nazionale Alpini in Milan, I found a drawer full of old photographs among which I immediately recognised two showing Mount Golico. "The sections send these war photographs to us, but we have no time to put them in order. We just leave them in that drawer," someone there said. "Take them if you want." The indifference of the Associazione to what so deeply had marked us survivors defies comment.

[12] The motto was in Friulano, the dialect spoken in Friuli, where the battalion was based and from where my Alpini originated.

[13] I met him again by chance in 1972 in Trieste, during an Alpino national reunion. I heard him exclaim: "Lieut Ferrante died years ago! It cannot possibly be him!" Somehow, he managed to avoid being sent to the Russian front and had gone back to his native Tarvisio. God knows how but he avoided the rest of the war.

[14] Three survivors of the *Galilea*, from left, Luciano Papinutti, Antonio Ferrante and Angelo Forte.

[15] Duca d'Aosta: the Duke of Aosta was the King of Italy's first cousin and one of the most respected commanders of the Italian armed forces. He led the fighting against the British in Ethiopia, dying as a prisoner of war in Nairobi, Kenya in 1942.

[16] Years later, in New York in 1948, I saw his sister Marie again on a visit to the USA. She told me that both her parents had died and the family had lost everything.

[17] NKVD: Translated as the People's Commisariat for Internal Affairs, or the secret police, forerunner of the KGB.

[18] Palmiro Togliatti: a member of the Italian Communist Party who fled to the USSR where he acquired Soviet citizenship and took an active part in the war effort against the Axis, in particular co-ordinating the action to "convert" Italian POW's to Communism. He was later repatriated to Italy, where he became a minister of state.

[19] "*Davaj, sabaka!*": Sabaka (dog) is the worst name a Russian can call someone.

---

[20] Kommandatura: The office of the political commissar, a member of State Security (NKVD) and the highest authority in the camp.

[21] Don Brevi: He was chaplain to the 9th Alpini in my Julia division and became a good friend. He was awarded the highest military decoration – the Medaglia d'Oro – during the Soviet offensive on the Don. During a sustained attack, the Russians had knocked out of action the two machine-gun nests defending his position. It was only a matter of moments before the Alpini were overrun and the Russians, who had already suffered large losses, were bound to extract revenge by executing any survivors. Don Brevi was the only surviving officer and had to choose quickly between his Christian faith and his men. He immediately took over one of the machine-guns and held the position, inflicting more losses on the Russians, until reinforcements arrived. The Vatican strongly objected to his being decorated, but to no avail.

[22] Gen Artur Schmidt: The deputy of Field Marshal Von Paulus during the battle of Stalingrad, Gen Schmidt was energetic and determined not to give up. He was reputed to have repeatedly intervened to stiffen Von Paulus' wavering morale. For more extensive information, refer to Anthony Beevor's book *Stalingrad* (translator's note).

[23] Gen Schmidt remained a prisoner in Siberian camps for a long time after the war but, unlike Von Paulus, never submitted to the Soviets. He was allowed to repatriate only in 1965, on the intercession of Chancellor Konrad Adenauer. The German government gave him a house and the services of an orderly.

[24] Italian émigrés: These Italian political exiles in the USSR were Communists or converted to Communism upon arrival. They were subsequently introduced among Italian POW's with the task of identifying suitable elements and converting them to the Soviet system.

[25] "Exoriare aliquis nostris ex ossibus ultor": Virgil, The Aeneid, book IV, verse 625. This verse is part of the curse uttered by Queen Dido who, on being abandoned by Aeneas, foresees the lasting enmity between her descendants (Carthage) and his (Rome). It is thought she was referring in particular to Hannibal.

[26] *Pirivochek* literally means interpreter. However, the few Italians fluent in Russian were generally those who had fled Fascist Italy and were employed by the Soviet authorities to liaise with prisoners, spy on them and hopefully convert them to Communism. The word had therefore acquired a pejorative connotation.

[27] After the war, it was said that his father disowned him.

[28] When I visited Gen Artur Schmidt in 1982, we both sang the song again. It was a moment of deep emotion and brotherly feeling.

[29] Italo Stagno was awarded the gold medal for military valour and died in a lager near Kiev in 1947 after a period in Siberia with a group of "recalcitrant" officers. Thirteen of these officers survived and were repatriated in 1954. In November 1946, shortly before dying, Stagno wrote a poem to his wife and daughter, born after his departure for the Russian front. The poem was smuggled out by Lieut Reginato, one of his companions. It reached Italy in 1954. This poem is included in *Vita Vissuta*, the Italian memoirs of Antonio Ferrante di Ruffano.

[30] Spain was neutral during the Second World War, but gave permission to volunteers to participate in the Russian campaign. They formed the Division Azul, which fought with distinction alongside us.

[31] The ineffectiveness of Italian authorities, always timid in pressing for information, didn't help either. They waited until 1999 before officially enquiring after the 200,000 soldiers who never returned from the Russian front.

[32] Later I got to know Palmieri better and we became friends. He recovered his mental health, became an MP and wrote the terrifying book *Davaj* on what happened in Soviet concentration camps.

[33] From then on, I remained much attached to the Prince, then King of Italy in his exile in Portugal. He always contacted me on his visits to Brussels, calling me Antonio, and once visited me in hospital.

[34] Thirty years later, I started yearly meetings at S. Margherita Ligure, near Portofino, where I founded the Order of the Kascia (*kasha* being the thin oatmeal soup that we POWs ate). The only people admitted were those who, as POWs, never betrayed their country to the Soviets. Early in the 21st century, we still meet every year, although few of us are left alive.

[35] Copyright: Vicentini, Carlo, *Noi Soli Vivi* (1997 and 2005), Gruppo Editoriale Mursia, Milan.